TENNIS

Let's Analyze Your Game

D0162211

by

Fred Stolle
**Former Grand Slam Champion
and Color Commentator for ESPN**

and

Bob Knight
Texas A & M University

Morton Publishing Company
925 W. Kenyon Ave., Unit 12
Englewood, Colorado 80110

Acknowledgments

We are appreciative of the contributions made by the following entities: *Tennis Magazine*, USTA, USPTA, ESPN, AAHPERD, and the Department of Health and Kinesiology at Texas A & M University.

We are most grateful to Bill Norris for sharing his professional expertise to improve amateur tennis. The knowledge presented will aid in keeping players healthy longer.

To Fred Mullane, we are particularly indebted for the professional photography.

During the photographic sessions, we utilized the finest playing equipment in the industry. This was made possible with the assistance of Nike, Sergio Tacchini, and FTM Sports.

Fred Stolle
Bob Knight

Foreword

by John Newcomb

Tennis books are not that easy to put together unless you have the knowledge and experience of someone like Fred Stolle.

Fred has virtually seen and done it all since he first travelled overseas in 1960.

As a product of the Australian post war coaching machine, which was regarded as the world's best in those years, Fred has expanded his knowledge to the point of being recognized as a true 'Grandmaster' in the world of tennis.

Technique is a real key to success and in this book Fred imparts, to the best of his ability, his knowledge of this important part of the game.

From being a first round loser in 1960, Fred moved over the years to the glory of Davis Cup and Grand Slam finals, a coach of greats such as Vitas Gerulaitis, and finally a world renown television commentator.

I wish him the best of luck with this book, knowing that it will really help people to further enjoy this 'game of a lifetime.'

Preface

We believe the simple style of instruction presented in this text is very practical in providing the skills and vivid expression of cues to become an exceptional performer. The methods allow the player to have fun and develop new skills. The instruction presented is based on sound psychological and bio-mechanical principles.

The variety of tests and drills may be self-administered; however, your professional will probably provide a more objective observation.

Behavioral objectives are included to enlighten player awareness of the outcomes expected. The book presents new ideas that encourage creativity for the player and professional. The tearout pages included provide for cognitive growth and prepare one for a progression of higher skill standards.

We have used these techniques to help thousands of players to learn more easily and win more consistently.

Table of Contents

1 Origin and History of Tennis   1

2 Choosing Your Equipment   7
Should I Invest in a Wide-Body?   8
Should I Use a Racket Press or Racket Cover?   9
What Is a Head-Heavy or Head-Light Racket? Which One Should I Use?   9
I Am Pretty Strong. Should I Use a Heavy Racket?   9
What Size Grip Do I Need?   10
I Can't Pay $300 For a Racket. How Can I Get a Good One Cheap?   11
Most Collegiate Players and Professionals Play with Cat Gut. What Kind Should I Buy?   11
Should My Racket Be Strung Tight or Loose?   12
How Will I Know If the Tension Is Correct?   12
What's the Difference Between Pressurized & Pressureless Balls? What Does Heavy-Duty Mean?   12
What Is the Best Tennis Shoe for Me?   12

3 Preventing Tennis Injuries   15
Blisters   16
Ankle Sprains   16
How To Avoid Tennis Elbow   17

4 As A Beginner, How Do I Start?   19
Expected Accomplishments   19
Pre-Test   21
Form Analysis Chart   27
As A Beginner, How Do I Start?   29
The Backswing, Footwork, and Follow-Through   31
Forehand Tips   34
Backhand Tips   34
Volleying Is Easy   35
Control the Serve   35
What's the Score?   38
Fun Games to Enhance Stroke Progression   44

5 The Intermediate and Advanced Player   49

Intermediate Tennis: Expected Accomplishments   49
Pre-Test   51
Form Analysis Chart   55
Advanced Tennis: Expected Accomplishments   57
Pre-Test — Advanced   59
Form Analysis Chart   63
The Forehand   65
The Backhand   67
The Two-Handed Player   68
The Approach Shot   69
Volley to Win   70
Successful Techniques for the Serve   73
Drop Shot   76
The Lob   77
The Overhead Smash   78
Singles Strategy   79
Doubles: Be Smart Like the Professional   82
Recreational Doubles   82

6 Drills and Skill Tests   85

Drills to Build Confidence   85
Skill Tests   88
Dyer Tennis Test   88
Broer-Miller Test   89
Kemp-Vincent Rally Test   90
Beginning Tennis Skills Test   917
Intermediate Tennis Skills Test   93

7 Special Topics   95

So You Want to Try the Western Forehand   95
The Left-Hander Has the Advantage   95
How to Watch Tennis   96
Mixed Doubles Can Be Fun   96
Playing Etiquette   97
Tennis Can Contribute to Your Well-Being   98
Program Your Concentration   99
Individual Goals and Team Enthusiasm   100
You Want to Change Your Game   101

Appendix   103

National Tennis Rating Program   103
Skill Problems   105
Introduction and Orientation for a Typical Tennis Class   108

Glossary of Terms   109
USTA Rules of Tennis   115

The Origin and History of Tennis

CHAPTER

1

A game similar to tennis has been played for approximately seven hundred years. Through evolution, tennis developed into the game we play today. Most historians credit France with originating the game of tennis. This early game was called "jeu de paume" because it was originally played with the palm of the hand. This older version of tennis is called "Court Tennis" in the U.S., "Real Tennis" in Great Britain and "Royal Tennis" in Australia to distinguish it from lawn tennis that developed in England in the nineteenth century.

Tennis was played by kings and knights in the castles and monasteries. The techniques, equipment, facilities and rules evolved over a three hundred year period into our family game of lawn tennis. It was played on a court 110 feet long, thirty-eight feet wide, and surrounded by four walls. The ball was played first with the hand, then with thong bindings, later with a paddle, and finally, late in the fifteenth or early sixteenth century, a racket. The first rules for tennis were written by a Frenchman, Forbet, in 1592. They were printed in 1599 and again in 1632.

There are still numerous mysteries associated with the development of tennis. The most convincing arguments for the name "tennis" is that the French word "tenez" was called out before serving. "Tenez" is a French deviation of the Latin word for "play." The scoring system is medieval, but it appears that the number sixty had a special significance in these early days. Sixty

1

was originally the winning score with each point equal to fifteen. Today, we have changed the third point, forty-five, to forty and simply called "game" at the fourth point rather than using sixty. "Love" probably meant "nothing." Some try to equate it with the French word "l'oeuf", meaning egg. The Americans generally use the term "goose egg." The theory indicates that "love" is a synonym for "nothing" may have originated from the expression "neither for love or money." "Service" was a term that developed because the Renaissance royalty used a servant to put the ball into play.

The early game of tennis reached its peak of popularity in both England and France in the sixteenth and seventeenth centuries. In the fourteenth century the masses began to play the game and made it a popular betting game. Edicts were passed prohibiting the playing of tennis, probably because of the gambling. Other times it was because playing tennis took away time from archery practice that was used for military purposes. Betting scandals became so widespread that the game nearly died in the eighteenth century. Wars and revolution helped to almost destroy tennis. The revival in popularity did not occur until early in the nineteenth century.

Court tennis was probably played in America for two hundred years before the introduction of "lawn tennis." Court tennis in America was a game played by the wealthy at private courts and exclusive clubs. It remained a popular game among the American elite until the depression of the 1930s, although there were never more than two dozen courts in the United States. Court tennis is virtually an unknown game in the U.S. today.

LAWN TENNIS   Although a version of the game of lawn tennis may have been played first by Major Harry Gem of England, it was his countryman, Major Walter Clopton Wingfield, who first patented the game and is recognized as the founder of lawn tennis. Walter C. Wingfield, a British army officer, introduced the game at an English lawn party in 1873. In 1874, he patented his game under the Greek name, "Sphairistike," which meant "ball game." His court was hourglass-shaped with a net four feet eight inches high in the middle. This game was first viewed in the same light as other lawn games such as croquet. It was seen as a game that could be played in one's finery and was appropriate for feminine play. "Sphairistike" grew in popularity very fast in spite of its cumbersome title. The name was soon shortened to "Sticky," and then simply "lawn tennis" which was the most apt description of the game. Lawn tennis surpassed croquet in popularity and almost immediately spread to all parts of the world.

A guest at Major Wingfield's lawn party was an army officer stationed in Bermuda. When he returned to Bermuda two weeks later, he took the game with him. Mary Ewing Outerbridge of Staten Island, New York, vacationed in Bermuda during January of 1874. While there, she saw the game played and became fascinated with it. Before sailing for home in February 1874, she purchased rackets and balls to take back to Staten Island. However, customs officials detained her and the tennis paraphernalia for a week. They did not know how to tax those strange implements. Later she introduced the game to the Staten Island Cricket and Baseball Club where her family held membership.

Tennis became popular among the Staten Island set. Most of Mary's girl friends shied away from the game because it took too much vigor and was not ladylike. Many of the young men were reluctant to play because the game had been introduced by a young woman. The term "love" used in tennis seemed to have feminine connotations as well. In spite of these early Victorian obstacles, the game continued to grow in popularity and spread beyond Staten Island and New York.

By 1880, some version of tennis was being played in many parts of the country. However, there were no standard rules, equipment, or scoring methods. E. H. Outerbridge, an older brother of Mary's, called a meeting in New York in 1881 of the leaders of all the eastern clubs where tennis was played. The purpose was to determine if standards could be established for the conduct of the game. This group adopted the rules of the All England Club to which we refer today as "Wimbledon." The United States National Lawn Tennis Association (USNLTA), the governing body for amateur tennis, was founded at this meeting. ("National" was dropped in 1920 and "Lawn" was dropped in 1975.)

The United States is divided into 17 geographic sections and all are governed by USTA. However, each is responsible for promoting and governing tennis in its area. Each competitive group is divided by sex and age: Youths under 12, 14, 16, 18 and 21; Men and women over 35, 50, 55, 60, 65 and 70; Men also have a

75 and 80 classification. Events include singles, doubles and sometimes mixed doubles. Some of the functions of USTA are noted below.

1. The USTA publishes and distributes the official rules in a yearly publication.

2. USTA conducts, supervises and sanctions both amateur and professional tournaments.

3. USTA establishes national rankings of U.S. players on the basis of participation in sanctioned tournaments.

4. USTA represents the U.S. in the International Tennis Federation.

5. USTA represents the U.S. on the Olympic committee, Pan American Games and the World University Games.

6. The USTA provides clinics, films, free materials, junior programs and numerous other services which benefit tennis.

DAVIS CUP   In 1900, Dwight F. Davis of St. Louis donated a cup for international men's play that served as an impetus for tennis. The Davis Cup is a tournament which, in the past, has symbolized international tennis supremacy. Dwight Davis, a Missourian, enrolled at Harvard and won the national doubles championship. It was at this time he originated the thought for international tennis competition. Britain was a logical opponent, because they considered themselves to be the best players in the world. So in 1900, Davis, with the approval of the USNLTA and the British, drew up a format that has never been changed. There would be two singles matches on the first day, a doubles match on the second day and the final two singles with the parings reversed on the final day. During the past eighty years, more than sixty-three countries have competed for the cup. This tournament is represented by men only.

WIGHTMAN CUP   The Wightman Cup was donated by Mrs. Hazel Hotchkiss Wightman in 1923 for women's international tennis as a counterpart of the Davis Cup. However, only the United States and Great Britain have ever played for the Wightman Cup. In 1963, the Federation Cup was inaugurated to meet the need for worldwide team competition for women.

World Championship Tennis (WCT) was formed in 1967 by Dave Dixon of New Orleans and Lamar Hunt of Dallas. This organization was to provide world class tournaments indoors. Prior to this time, professional tournaments exhibited little direction, except to make a profit. The appointment of a knowledgeable young business executive, Al Hill, Jr. as President, was the beginning of a force that dramatically changed tennis.

Early battles with the International Lawn Tennis Federation (ILTF) caused growth to develop slowly. ILTF was "afraid the taint of professionalism would damage its prestige." Additional troubles developed when traditional tennis enthusiasts were angered with WCTs introduction of colorful tennis attire worn by professionals. Historically, only white clothing was allowed on club and private courts.

The success WCT achieved with television contracts changed this public ire to player and spectator enthusiasm. Many believe this TV coverage to be the catalyst for the tennis boom of the seventies.

The first players to sign contracts were John Newcomb, Tony Roche, Cliff Drysdale, Nikki Pilic, Dennis Ralston, Butch Buckholz, Pierre Barthes, and Roger Taylor. These players were called the "Handsome Eight," or as Fred Stolle says, the "Handsome Seven" and Tony Roche. WCT disbanded in August 1990.

The Federation Cup provides international team competition for women. It was established in 1963. One nation plays another (two singles, one doubles) in a single elimination tournament at one sight during one week.

Founded in December 1968 in Dallas, Texas, The Maureen Connolly Brinker Tennis Foundation came into existence as a tribute to this outstanding young woman and tennis player. Nancy Jeffett and Maureen's husband, Norman, established the foundation to raise money for the development of junior girls tennis. These efforts resulted in the tremendous upsurge of talent representing women's tennis today.

In 1972, The Association of Tennis Professionals (ATP) was formed with forty players. Jack Kramer served as the first executive director. Today, almost 1,000 members are assured the best possible conditions in which to follow their profession. Players can gain ATP membership in the Division I category by being

WORLD CHAMPIONSHIP TENNIS (WCT)

FEDERATION CUP

MAUREEN CONNOLLY BRINKER TENNIS FOUNDATION

ASSOCIATION OF TENNIS PROFESSIONALS

ranked among the top 200 in the world on the ATP singles computer ranking. A more recent Division II category opens eligibility to players ranked 501-1000 on the singles computer and 1–500 in doubles.

The International Tennis Weekly, the official newspaper of the ATP, is the major information outlet for news in pro tennis. ATP members wrote the code of conduct in 1976. ATP now has offices in Jacksonville, New York and Paris.

IBM - ATP International Business Machines has developed a co-sponsorship with the Association of Tennis Professionals to play seventy-four international tournaments each year. Forty-four million dollars in prize money will be distributed to the participants. Qualifications for entry is based on ATP computer rankings. Each tournament will allow some qualifiers and some wild card entries. Grand Slam events are not included in the tournament schedule.

Choosing Your Equipment

CHAPTER 2

- ▶ Should I buy a wood, metal or composite racket?
- ▶ What's the difference anyway?
- ▶ What about an oversized racket?
- ▶ Are the wide-bodies any good?

Choosing new equipment should be pure pleasure for the tennis player. It serves as an opportunity to be exposed to new information and technology. A number of sporting goods stores provide highly crafted rackets as demonstrators. You can decide what feels good as you hit the ball. Is the head too heavy? Is the grip just right? Is it springy or stiff? Be comfortable with your choice, but remember, equipment alone won't make you a champion by the weekend.

There are several kinds of materials used to make tennis rackets. They are wood, ceramic, kevelar, graphite, boron, aluminum, fiberglass, twaron and composites. Wood rackets are generally crafted with laminations of different woods, combining the properties of durability, hardness, lightness and springiness. Overlays of fiber may be bonded to all or part of the frame. Rackets made chiefly of boron or graphite are usually very stiff. The open throat of two-shafted rackets are usually more flexible longitudinally. This design offers greater resistance to twisting or torquing when the ball is hit. Those who prefer a stiffer racket may choose the same frame design with a hard metal piece in the cross section of the throat. This prevents the shafts from moving independently and reduces torque.

What this gobbledygook means is a racket with a flexible shaft and a stiff head favors the ground stroker's game, and a stiff shaft and flexible head favors the server's game.

The mid-sized and oversized racket have become the standard. The stigma, that it is an old man's racket has passed. The hitting area is 10-50 percent greater than the old standard rackets. Volleys and groundstrokes theoretically improve one's accuracy.

SHOULD I INVEST IN A WIDE-BODY?

The development of the wide-body is the most dramatic change in racket technology since the switch from wood to hi-tech composites. It is just as dramatic as the change from traditional size heads to oversized heads. Tracy Leonard, equipment advisor, indicates that this new technology has given racket engineers considerable design latitude. It allows them to create more variance in racket playability than ever before.

The basic concept of the wide-body is to build a racket that performs more efficiently, that transfers more of the energy of the collision between the ball and the strings back into the shot. The more a racket flexes or bends back longitudinally at impact, the less energy your shot gets from that collision. The way to keep a racket from bending is to make it stiffer, and increased stiffness translates into more power. In simple terms, the racket does more of the work for the player.

With previous racket changes, designers moved from wood to metal to fiberglass and, finally, graphite, which is stiff and light. They reached a point where stiffness could not be increased without sacrificing comfort. As a result, experimentation with the shape and size of the racket's cross section produced a new dimension. This new curved, aerodynamic, wider body allows the engineer to manipulate the stiffness of the frame and create different playability characteristics in different areas of the racket.

Generally, where a racket is widest is where it is stiffest and where it is thinner it is more flexible. The purpose of the engineered flex is to absorb the shock of the ball's impact before it reaches the arm.

Because of the expanded dimensions, many wide-bodies look more bulky than traditional frames, but they are not harder to swing. Many are easier to swing. The walls of air or foam filled wide-body frames are very thin. Some are lighter than traditional frames.

What has a more profound effect on maneuverability than overall weight and shape is the location of the widest point of the racket. That is usually the area of greatest weight. If the majority of weight is near where you hold it, it will be easier to swing. However, if the weight is at the tip of the head, it will be harder to swing.

Today's wide-bodies offer a bigger range of power, control, maneuverability, and shock dampening than previous rackets.

SHOULD I USE A RACKET PRESS OR RACKET COVER?

Presses were extensively used when all rackets were wood and crafted with wood laminations. Today's rackets do not need a press. Racket covers protect gut strings from humidity and are used by most players.

WHAT IS A HEAD-HEAVY OR HEAD-LIGHT RACKET? WHICH ONE SHOULD I USE?

Place a strung racket on a fulcrum at exactly midpoint between the top of the head and the butt. Is it head heavy, center balanced or head light? The head heavy racket puts more mass into the ball at impact. This may cause tiring in long matches. Center balance and head light rackets usually promote a natural arm flow and help put pace on the ball. The feel of the swing is a prime consideration. The wide-bodies tend to neutralize the head weight more than standard mid-, or oversized rackets.

I AM PRETTY STRONG. SHOULD I USE A HEAVY RACKET?

Less than 2 ounces separate a light from a heavy. The light frame is usually 10–11 ounces; the medium is 11–12, ounces and anything above is heavy. The string will add about ½ ounce. Cheap rackets often weigh less than 10 ounces. Few professionals use a heavy. Most use a medium. But they play every day and possess tremendous arm strength. A male should consider a frame between 11–13 ounces. A female should consider 10–12½ ounces.

WHAT SIZE GRIP DO I NEED? Racket grips generally range from four to five inches. Four ways to determine your grips are:

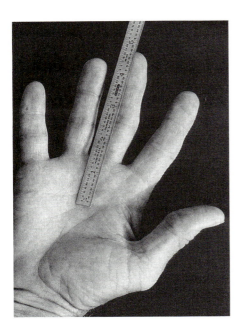

1. Measure the distance from the longitudinal crease in your palm. Measure to the tip of your ring finger. Place the ruler between the ring finger and middle finger. The distance observed should be a comfortable circumference for you.

2. Hold the racket with an Eastern forehand grip. (See Figure 4.1.) Place your fingers around the grip. The end of the thumb should touch the first joint of the middle finger.

3. Play with a demo racket. Look for comfort and an easy to swing racket. If your hand or arm tire quickly, the grip or weight may suggest that you try a different size grip or a different weight racket.

Aluminum rackets and traditional style rackets are less expensive than composites and wide-bodies. General price ranges for rackets are:

Standard mid-sized or oversized

Wood	$ 35–60
Aluminum	$ 80–150
Graphite, fiber glass composite	$100–140
Graphite, ceramic, boron composite	$150–250

Wide-bodies

Graphite, fiberglass composite	$100–150
Graphite, ceramic composite	$100–250
Graphite, kevelar composite	$175–225
Graphite, twaron fiberglass composite	$225–275

Search for the best buy. Look for that special deal on last year's models. Compare prices and services offered by that particular shop. Inquire about racket warranty.

I CAN'T PAY $300 FOR A RACKET. HOW CAN I GET A GOOD ONE CHEAP?

Players who use gut, play with lamb, sheep or beef gut, not cat gut. Gut plays beautifully, and grips the ball better, but is subject to dampness from humidity. It is very expensive and lasts only a short time. It is constructed in three gauges, 15, 16 and 17. Seventeen is the thinnest and wears quickly. Play with gut only if your rating is a 4.0 or above (see rating scale on page 91).

Nylon string is much cheaper and is made with numerous characteristics and in many colors.

"Oil impregnated" nylon is lubricated to develop resiliency and ease of stringing.

"Oil filled" string is hollow and contains an oil that is trapped by plugs at the end of the string. The moving action of the oil reduces distortion at impact. Artificial gut or synthetic gut is actually nylon or new space-age polymers spun and bound together to simulate natural gut. These are Kevelar and Zyex. Zyex is the most recent new material and is used as a center core for strings. It is reported to provide resiliency, elasticity and more power. Many string manufacturers indicate that it retains tension and plays better than any other synthetic.

Any of these strings can be used in a wide-body frame.

MOST COLLEGIATE PLAYERS AND PROFESSIONALS PLAY WITH CAT GUT. WHAT KIND SHOULD I BUY?

Monofilament and multifilament have long durability and are inexpensive. However, they do not play "with feel."

SHOULD MY RACKET BE STRUNG TIGHT OR LOOSE?

Tight strings produce more control. Loose strings give more speed and power. Most manufacturers include string tension recommendations in a booklet with a new racket. Should recommendations not be included, a certified racket stringer will know the specific stringing characteristics of the frame. He/she will also be able to string it to help improve your own playing characteristics.

HOW WILL I KNOW IF THE TENSION IS CORRECT?

Most pros can judge the string tension by sound and feel. Unfortunately, club players usually do not play enough to make a sound judgement of tension. The most widely used machines to test tension, balance, or stiffness are made by Babolat and are found in most pro shops.

WHAT'S THE DIFFERENCE BETWEEN PRESSURIZED AND PRESSURELESS BALLS? WHAT DOES HEAVY-DUTY MEAN?

Any USTA approved ball with rebound between 53-58 inches when dropped (on a standard surface) from a height of 100 inches is a heavy-duty ball.

Pressurized balls have an internal air pressure of about 15 pounds per square inch.

Pressureless balls have a thicker core and have a heavy feel when ball impact occurs. The durability is much better than pressurized balls. Pressureless balls are used at high altitudes to compensate for the thinner air.

Heavy-duty balls have a different rubber and nap formula which gives longer service on abrasive surfaces. An extremely abrasive surface causes a "fuzzing" which makes it harder to play a "finesse game".

USTA approved balls will cost from $2.00–$4.00, depending on where they are purchased.

WHAT IS THE BEST TENNIS SHOE FOR ME?

Fit

When you put the shoes on make sure they fit well. They should not feel as though they need to be "broken in" for a few days. Ian Hamilton of Nike states that "a good tennis shoe must be built on an anatomically correct last so the shoe's base of support helps the foot to remain stable in the shoe."

A lightweight shock-absorbing shoe that protects against stress related injuries will reduce the feeling of tiredness on the court.

Comfort

A number of manufacturers have developed "high tops" to increase ankle support. Special materials are used for ankle and forefoot support and new space-age material for shock absorption. A strap on the forefoot or mediallateral speed lacing allows for increased midfoot stability.

Stability

Polyurethane, Indy 500-Plus, Endura Rubber, and Durathane are only a few of the new outsole materials manufacturers are using to make shoes last three to five times longer.

Durability

It is evident in the marketplace that players want a high fashion classic shoe. Manufacturers would prefer not to change colors and models every six months. However, today's tennis player demands a shoe that stays clean and white and promotes a confident self-image.

Cosmetics

High fashion, high tech shoes that have been researched and developed to meet your needs will cost more than "sneakers." Expect to pay $70–$100 for this new styling, highly technical, and durable shoe.

Price

CHAPTER

Preventing Tennis Injuries

by Bill Norris

During my years as head trainer for some of the top professionals in the world, I am amazed that so few injuries occur, considering the heavy playing schedule. The primary reason for the reduced injuries is the outstanding playing condition of these athletes.

Correct technique in stroking the ball is one preventive measure to reduce muscle stress and pain. A player should hit the ball so the force transfer moves from the racket to the arm to the shoulder and body. Poor mechanics will load too much stress on the bones, joints, ligaments, tendons and muscles.

Weekend or club players sometime develop trauma in connective tissue which holds the musculoskeletal system together. This generally occurs because of poor conditioning of the muscular system. Because tennis requires short bursts of intense activity and is then followed by a pause in activity, cardiorespiratory training is also vital.

Quick starts and stops will occasionally cause gastrocnemius (calf) strain. The athlete makes a quick stop with the foot planted flat-footed and quickly extends the knee. This places enormous stress on the medial head of the gastrocnemius. This type of injury can usually be prevented by normal achilles tendon stretching. If pain continues, use a gentle ice massage. Later, use a gentle, gradual-stretch routine. Follow-up includes cold, heat, mild exercise and walking in low-heeled shoes. If pain is severe, consult a physician.

Few amateur tennis players warm up properly. Have you ever watched a sprinter, a gymnast or a college wrestler warm up? The professional tennis player will often warm up an hour or more before a match. Yet the weekend player will stroke a few balls and believe he is ready to go 100%.

Your warm-up should include light jogging, stretching, light calisthenics, flexibility and agility movement. This warm-up stretches the connective tissue which tightens up during rest and gets the player ready to consume more oxygen. It develops neuromuscular readiness which reduces flex time. This gets a player ready psychologically. An active player should use both isometric and isotonic exercises. Legs, shoulders, and upper body will be strengthened enough to reduce most injuries.

BLISTERS

The racket-hand and feet are often sources of tenderness after a long lay-off. Sometimes a worn grip or incorrect size of racket handle causes problems. Ask a pro to help you size a grip. Cheap socks and poorly fitted shoes may be the cause of blisters on the feet. An area can become inflamed with fluid under the skin. In this case, the area should be kept clean. If the skin gets broken, antibacterial ointment should be used. A thin piece of foam rubber with a small round hole cut to fit the inflamed area will often reduce pain in the injured area.

ANKLE SPRAINS

Ankle sprains can sometimes be reduced by stretching the Achilles tendon, stretching the muscles, and wearing the correct shoes.

Most tennis sprains are developed by the sudden lateral or medial twist and damages ligaments and tendons.

When treating a sprain:

1. Stop play and determine if the ankle is stable or unstable.
2. Apply an elastic bandage to reduce internal bleeding.
3. Apply ice immediately for a twenty minute period. Apply five-six times a day.
4. Elevate the leg.

Alternating heat and ice can begin the third day if hemorrhaging has stopped. If there is a possibility of a fracture refer to a physician.

The condition may result from stress, overuse or a combination of both. Normally, the stresses are induced because the muscles involved in tennis skills are not adequately developed to meet the demands. The stress may be acute or may result from a chronic condition. Examples of incorrect tennis fundamentals which may contribute to this condition are: hitting the ball late, using wrist action, improper backhand or incorrect serve procedures. The injury may not have developed from tennis. The arm may have been hit or there may be overuse of the hand and forearm. Hammering nails, using a screw driver, washing dishes or shaking hands could contribute to this excruciating pain.

One of the conditions that develops is pain along the inside or outside of the elbow which is the medial and lateral epicondyle of the humerus. You can diagnose the pain more easily by observing Figure 3-1. The supinator muscle runs along the lateral epicondyle where there is an aponeurotic or tendon attachment. This irritation develops where the tendon attaches to the bone. The carpal extensor muscles must contract to stabilize the wrist, therefore any gripping or clenching of a racket is difficult when there is tenderness in the elbow.

The primary treatment is *rest* with a prescribed treatment program. Physicians, trainers and physical therapy technicians are best equipped to evaluate this problem. Generally, two to four weeks of rest from activities using the hand and forearm is sufficient. Other factors listed may be beneficial in reducing pain. Apply an ice pack over the tender area following your match. Consider changing to a racket that absorbs more shock. String your racket with less tension. Ask a qualified professional to observe your strokes. Keep the arm warm with a jacket or sweater until the muscles are relaxed. Occasionally, an elastic band around the forearm offers relief to some players. Scientific data does not support the use of a copper bracelet.

A preventative program is the wise decision in combating this ailment. I recommend a weight program to strengthen the muscles of the forearm. Observe in Figure 3-1 the range of motion used with the light weights.

▶ Begin with 2 or 5-pound plate. Adjust up or down after first day's workout — add 1, or 2+ pounds on the first workout day of each week.

▶ Hold arms at shoulder level with hands (knuckles up) near center of the bar.

HOW TO AVOID TENNIS ELBOW

Figure 3-1.
How to avoid tennis elbow.

1. Release left hand only — turn bar away from you, as shown, with right hand.
2. Grip bar with left hand, release right hand, and turn bar away from you.
3. Continue this until the plate touches the bar.
4. Reverse the hand action until the chain is extended.

▶ This is one (1) repetition.
▶ Do three (3) reps without stopping.
▶ Do three sets during a workout. Place this exercise where you desire, spacing the three sets evenly throughout the program.
▶ Do this at a moderate rate of speed.
▶ Do not start with too much weight. It is the full manipulation of the hands and wrists that is important. The bar should be held at shoulder level.

The little finger should remain in contact with the bar at all times.

Movement 1
From the above starting position lower bar forward (keeping small finger in contact and elbow in flexed position). Stop, raise bar upward and backward as far as you can, keeping small finger in contact and hand clenched. Return to starting position. This is one repetition. Continue movements to ten reps.

Movement 1

Figure 3-1.
How to avoid tennis elbow
(continued).

Movement 2
From the above position lower bar slowly to the right horizontal position. Stop. Raise bar to starting position. Stop. This is the count of one. From this position lower slowly to the left horizontal position. Stop. Then return to the starting position. This is the count of two (stop at the top each time). Continue these movements until you have completed ten reps in each direction (a total of 20).

Movement 3
Lower bar forward. Stop. Circling the bar from this position to the right, moving the hand and wrist only until the bar moves to the forward position. Stop. This is repetition number one. Reverse the movement toward the left and in a counter-clockwise movement until the forward position is reached. Stop. This is repetition number two. Continue movements until the count reaches 20.

As A Beginner, How Do I Start?

CHAPTER

4

At the completion of this unit the player should be able to accomplish the following:

1. List two reasons to adopt the ready position.

2. Enumerate at least two playing differences between the eastern forehand and western forehand grip.

3. Discuss three reasons why the baseline player should hit the ball at least three feet over the net.

4. Recognize the server's or receiver's court position based on the game score.

5. Identify and define twenty tennis terms found in the glossary.

6. Mimic the three movements for volleying and successfully hit three of five balls into the opposing court.

7. Mimic correctly the positions established for the beginning serve and successfully hit two of five balls into the correct court.

8. Rally a ball from the baseline 50 percent more times than at the beginning of the instruction.

PRE-TEST — BEGINNER

Name _____ Date _____

Section _____ Time _____

Before you read any of the material in this section, take the pre-test to determine if you need to read the information.

Match the following. Place the correct letter in the space provided.

_____	1. Match	A.	Three of five games
		B.	Server ahead by one point after deuce
_____	2. Game	C.	Each player has two points
		D.	Score of a player with no points
_____	3. Set	E.	Smallest scoring unit
		F.	Winning six games, ahead by two
_____	4. 30 All	G.	Receiver ahead by one point after deuce
		H.	Term used to describe a tie score of 40–40
_____	5. Ad In	I.	Two of three sets
		J.	Winning four points, ahead by at least two
_____	6. Ad Out	K.	Served ball falls into incorrect area
		L.	Line at each end of the court
_____	7. Point	M.	Mid line running from alley to alley
		N.	No man's land
_____	8. Love	O.	Point played over because of interference
		P.	Areas outside singles line
_____	9. Deuce		
_____	10. Fault		
_____	11. Let		
_____	12. Baseline		
_____	13. Back Court		
_____	14. Alley		
_____	15. Service Line		

Place T for True and F for False in the space provided.

_____ 1. Player calling out score calls receiver's score first.

_____ 2. A game score of 5-40 is correct if server has one point and receiver three points.

_____ 3. A ball landing on the sideline boundary is good.

_____ 4. A server's foot may not touch the baseline until ball contact is made.

_____ 5. The suggested grip for most players is the Eastern.

_____ 6. Players change ends of the court at the completion of games two, four, six, eight, etc.

_____ 7. In a doubles match either player may return serves during the game.

_____ 8. The transfer of weight for any stroke occurs just after the racket head meets the ball.

_____ 9. Closing the face of the racket should cause the ball to move downward.

_____ 10. When hitting the forehand or backhand shot the racket head should be swung toward the ground.

_____ 11. In certain instances the ball may be returned legally after it has bounced twice.

_____ 12. A game score of 6-5 indicates the set is over.

_____ 13. Two serves are allowed to get the ball in the proper serving area.

_____ 14. A common reason for hitting the ball into the net is due to slow racket preparation.

_____ 15. The ball should be held in the palm of the hand during the service toss.

_____ 16. The ready position requires the head of one's racket to be pointed at the opponent's feet.

_____ 17. Most collegiate and professional tournaments use the 12 point tiebreaker rather than the 9 point tiebreaker.

_____ 18. The backswing should not exceed 180 degrees.

_____ 19. In "no ad." scoring, when the score is tied at 3 points all, the server has the choice into which court the seventh point will be served.

_____ 20. VASSS is a name for no ad scoring.

_____ 21. Deuce indicates that each player has two points.

_____ 22. In doubles, the player serving should stand as close to the center mark as possible.

_____ 23. In doubles play, one should hit toward the alley when possible, because of the percentage value of the shot.

_____ 24. One can successfully use the continental or backhand grip when serving.

_____ 25. A good baseline player almost always hits the ball more than one foot over the net.

Choose the best answer. Place the correct letter in the space provided.

_____ 1. Most historians credit which of the following countries with originating tennis.
   A.   U.S.A.
   B.   England
   C.   France
   D.   Australia

_____ 2. The game was first titled
   A.   jeu de paume
   B.   Love
   C.   Handball
   D.   Service

_____ 3. The game was patented by
   A.   Jack Kramer
   B.   Mary Outerbridge
   C.   Hazel Wightman
   D.   Walter Wingfield

_____ 4. World Championship Tennis (WCT)
   A.   Develops world class tournaments
   B.   Supports the International Lawn Tennis Federation
   C.   Classifies all professional players
   D.   Has disbanded and ceases to exist

_____ 5. The Association of Tennis Professionals (ATP)
   A.   Ranks professional players
   B.   Ranks all tournament players
   C.   Controls all professional tournaments
   D.   Makes policy for international tennis

_____ 6. The Davis Cup is a tournament designed for
   A.   National tournaments
   B.   International Competition
   C.   Competition between the U.S. and Britain
   D.   Competition between men and women

_____ 7. The Wightman Cup was formed in 1923 by:
   A.   Nancy Jeffett
   B.   Hazel Hotchkiss
   C.   Billie Jean King
   D.   Greta Garbo

_____ 8. The Davis Cup is an international tournament that:
   A. Has served as an impetus for tennis in more than sixty countries
   B. Restricts play to the U.S. and England
   C. Allows men and women to serve as goodwill ambassadors
   D   Places amateurs against professionals

_____ 9. ATP is:
   A. A special oil for tennis strings
   B. The governing body for professional tennis
   C. A new space-age polymer
   D. A tennis magazine

_____ 10. The Brinker Foundation:
   A. Trains umpires and linesman
   B. Governs tennis in the southwest U.S.
   C. Arbitrates conflicts between mens and womens tennis
   D. Funds junior programs for girls

_____ 11. Following most shots
   A. Return to the middle of the court
   B. Return to the middle of the baseline
   C. Wait to see where your opponent's next shot will hit
   D. Move to the net

_____ 12. Which of the following coaching cues applies primarily to the volley?
   A. Hit up and out — over the ball
   B. Swing from low to high
   C. Take the racket back early
   D. Turn-step-block

_____ 13. All factors being equal, the following would be the best choice in selecting a racket.
   A. Wood — 70–75 inches
   B. Aluminum — 90–100 inches
   C. Wood — 90–100 inches
   D. Composite — 90–105 inches

_____ 14. What is the meaning of the term "ACE"?
   A. The server won the point
   B. The first serve was a good serve
   C. The receiver was unable to return a good serve
   D. The receiver was unable to reach a good serve

_____ 15. What is it called when a ball is returned immediately after its bounce?

   A. A volley
   B. A drop volley
   C. A half volley
   D. A groundstroke

_____ 16. Stepping forward on volleys provides:

   A. Power
   B. Control
   C. Both a and b
   D. Neither a or b

_____ 17. Where should the service be made when the score is 40 love?

   A. From the right side of the court
   B. From the left side of the court
   C. From either side depending upon the side from which the game was started
   D. The receiver determines the side

_____ 18. In the 12 point tie breaker, when do players change ends of the court?

   A. Never
   B. After the first point is played
   C. After two points are played
   D. After six points are played

_____ 19. When playing a baseline game, what should the players positions be?

   A. About 3 feet behind the baseline
   B. Right on the baseline
   C. Between the baseline and the service line
   D. Halfway between the baseline and net

_____ 20. Which of the answers below best represent a defensive stroke against a net player?

   A. Drop shot
   B. Slice drive
   C. Lob
   D. Volley

_____ 21. If a player is unable to determine if a ball is in or out, the correct choice should be:

   A. Call it out
   B. Ask to play a "let"
   C. Call it good
   D. Ask your opponent if he/she saw it hit

____ 22. If a tossed ball is swung at and missed on the first serve:
   A. Take the serve over
   B. It's a lost point for the server
   C. It's a fault
   D. It does not count

____ 23. At the beginning of a match, the winner of the coin toss or racket spin may choose all of the following EXCEPT:
   A. Choose only to serve, receive, or end of court
   B. Choose to serve or receive
   C. Ask opponent to choose
   D. Choose to serve and choose end of court

____ 24. A player standing beyond the baseline catches the ball.
   A. Player catching the ball loses the point
   B. You play a let
   C. Player catching ball wins the point (it was already past the baseline)
   D. Player hitting the ball loses the point

____ 25. On a questionable call, who makes the final decision?
   A. The players
   B. The coach
   C. You play it over
   D. Any spectator who saw the point

Name _____

Section _____

Time _____ Date _____

Form Analysis Chart

	Observation #1	Observation #2	Evaluation	
				Place the appropriate number in the space provided for the specific skill or movement.

Professional or near perfect   _5_

Outstanding   _4_

Average   _3_

Needs Improving   _2_

Poor   _1_

SERVE

Correct grip ....

Comfortable stance ....

Toe pointed correctly ....

Accurate toss...............................

Chin up ....

Adequate weight change..............

Rhythmic backswing ....

Full backswing ....

Racket arm extended at impact ....

Hitting up and out.......................

Follow-through ....

Backfoot across the baseline.........

Ball control ....

FOREHAND

Eastern forehand ....

Return to ready position ....

Racket preparation ....

Correct footwork.........................

Swing ....

Ball contact ....

Weight transfer............................

Follow-through ....

Ball control ....

Add the totals and observe the chart below to categorize your form.

Professional or near perfect	175-190 points
Advanced amateur or more successes than errors	150-174 points
Hacker or more errors than successes	100-124 points
Inept or many more errors than successes	75-99 points

(Continued)

	Observation #1	Observation #2	Evaluation
BACKHAND			
Eastern backhand			
Return to ready position			
Racket preparation			
Correct footwork			
Swing			
Ball contact			
Weight transfer			
Follow-through			
Ball control			
VOLLEY			
Correct grip			
Shoulder turned			
Step correctly			
Ball contact in front			
Body low during ball contact			
Uses forehand and backhand			
Ball control			
Total			

Grand Total Evaluation _____

To improve technique, read sections relating to specific skills.

"I don't know where I'm supposed to go when I get on the court." "When I get there, I'll look silly with that racket of mine." These thoughts are common for many beginners to tennis.

Our daily activity includes walking, and because we can perform this function, balance is pretty well assured. Therefore, footwork is an easy technique to master. The ready position can be accomplished immediately. In this position the player bends at the knees and the waist. This should be a comfortable position which allows the player to feel flexible. This position should be taken with the player facing the direction of the opponent. The feet should be about shoulder width apart with the weight spread evenly on the balls of the feet. Quick stops and starts can be made from this position. The novice player will not have that feeling of looking like a beginner after practicing this technique with a critical observer.

Racket control begins by selecting the proper grip and developing a feel of the ball hitting the strings. Get a ball and racket and bounce the ball up and down on the surface. Contact the ball on the center of the strings. Place the racket at a different angle and bounce it a few times. Do you think it's too difficult? Just remember, the strings are flat, and the ball bounces in a direction equal to the angle of the racket face. This occurs when playing a game. When the strings are angled up, the ball goes up. When the strings are angled down, the ball goes down.

When we accept this concept we can quickly adapt to the standard Eastern grip used by the majority of the top amateurs and professional players (Figure 4-1). This is the "shake hands" grip. Learn this grip by placing the palm of your hand on the racket face and slide it down to the lower part of the grip. Or make a "V" between the forefinger and the thumb. A right handed player will place the "V" over the bevel on the top right hand side.

To obtain the Eastern Backhand grip, simply turn the racket hand one quarter turn counter clockwise from the eastern forehand (Figure 4-2). This will place the knuckle of the index finger on top of the handle. Spread the fingers to cover the greatest area of the handle, or place the "V" over the bevel on the top left hand side.

Another method of finding the backhand grip is to make a fist with the thumb extended. Use this same procedure and grip a racket with the thumb behind the racket face. Have a partner toss

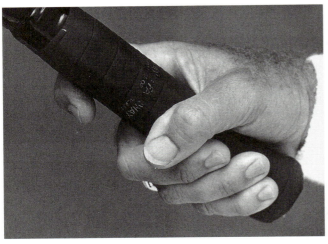

Figure 4-1. Eastern forehand.

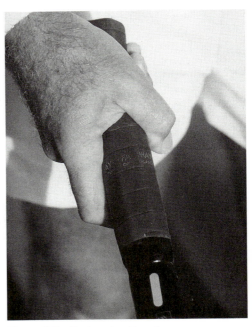

Figure 4-2. Eastern backhand.

a ball toward you. The ball contact is made with the face of the racket. The same skill is accomplished when you hold the racket halfway down the shaft, then all way down to the leather grip. Practice each of these routines with the forehand and backhand grip to become comfortable.

You will stand at the ready position using the forehand grip. This grip is switched only when the ball is hit to the opposite side.

1. Hold the racket with the forehand grip. Stand in the ready position (Figure 4-3). Using the free hand, gently hold the throat of the racket at about 45 degrees from the court.

2. When the ball comes to the forehand, simply bring the racket back 180 degrees on the same side (Figure 4-4).

3. When the ball comes to the backhand, change the grip to the backhand as you are bringing the racket back to the same 180 degrees. The free hand lifting the throat of the racket allows the quick change to be made.

Figure 4-3. Ready position.

Figure 4-4. Bring the racket back 180° on the same side.

THE BACKSWING, FOOTWORK, AND FOLLOW-THROUGH

Forehand & Backhand — Quick Success

Early racket preparation contributes positively to the complete stroke. The backswing should begin as the ball leaves the opponent's racket. This procedure allows enough time to successfully hit the ball. You react more rhythmically with a fluid backswing. This early preparation gives you enough time to move toward the ball and establish the most desirable body alignment and footwork.

The foot opposite the racket side is moved toward the net. The non-hitting shoulder is at a right angle to the net. The pivoting of the racket shoulder actually takes the racket arm back to the half-way or 180 degree position. Ball contact is made as the weight transfers to the leading foot. The point of contact is slightly in front and to the side of the leading foot. Ball contact should be made at waist level. When the ball is lower, just flex the knees to lower the body. Observe Figure 4-5.

To obtain optimum results from this effort, allow the racket to move forward and up after ball contact. (See Figure 4-6.) The upper arm will be near the chin on a good follow-through. This is the stroking action that gives the ball direction, control, and

Figure 4-5. For a lower ball, just flex the knees.

Figure 4-6. Allow the racket to move forward and up after ball contact.

pace. This is the action that helps a player to develop the feel that successful tennis players talk about. By mastering these fundamentals, the most inept player can develop an accurate and powerful groundstroke.

Forehand & Backhand — Quick Success

The most successful tennis players at any level of play are those who use the same routine with each shot. The correct shot imaged in your thought becomes very efficient after thousands of hits.

The backswing, pivot, ball contact, and follow-through are developed naturally using these methods.

Racket preparation is a key and can be mastered in a few sessions. As your opponent hits the ball, take your racket back and move to the ball. Make the hit just in front of and to the side of your leading foot. Stay low during the process so more power and accuracy will be delivered.

Side-Shuffle, Left and Right. The movement is similar to that used in basketball. A player moves sideways in a skipping motion. Many shots require movement of about six to ten feet from the original ready position. In moving to the right, you first push off with the left foot by picking up the right foot and moving it to the right. Put the weight on the right foot and then quickly pick up the left foot and place it alongside the right foot. You then repeat the movement.

In moving to the left or the left foot would be moved first and the right foot would then be placed alongside of it.

Two or three steps in each direction, alternately, make a good routine.

When executing a smash, you may not always be able to hit the ball with both feet on the ground. Should this occur, push off the right foot as the racket is moved to the front of you, leap up and land on the left foot. This movement is the scissors kick.

Cross-Over Step, Left and Right. The player turns from the ready position (facing the sideline) as in actual play. If a right-hander turns to the right for a forehand, he pivots on the right foot and swings the left across the front of the body and steps outward toward the net, putting the weight on the left foot, then returns to the ready position after the shot.

In turning to the left, the right foot is crossed over in front of the body.

The two movements can be combined for forehand and backhand turning alternately. They can be combined with a side-shuffle, or two side-shuffles followed quickly by a cross-over step.

Forward Shuffle, Forehand and Backhand. The forward shuffle is used in actual play to move forward about six or eight feet to play a short ball. It combines the quick cross-over step and a side shuffle, but the movement of the body is forward, toward the net. For a ball on the right, the initial cross-over movement is toward the right; for balls on the left, the movement is toward the left. The left foot would be leading in the forward shuffle (toward the net) for forehands, and the right for backhands.

Backward Shuffle for the Right-Hander Playing a Forehand and Backhand. This backhand shuffle is used to play a deep ball, for which the player must move back about six to eight feet. For a

Footwork for Winning Play

forehand, the player pivots away from the net, on his left foot, as he swings his right foot backward away from the net.

For backhands, the pivot is made on the right foot as the left foot is swung backward, away from the net, and the left foot leads in the backward shuffle.

The backward shuffle can be combined with the forehand shuffle to comprise a good practice routine.

Oblique (Angle) Running, Left and Right. Oblique running is used in actual play when a ball is far enough from a player to require actual running to it, rather than merely shuffling or cross-stepping to it. Use this drill from the ready position. Run in the general direction of the net post. Six or seven steps are all that are generally required, after which the player stops in a position to play an imaginary forehand or backhand. The player would run toward the right net post for a forehand and finish with his body in a sideways hitting position, with the left foot forward. For a backhand, the player would run toward the left net post and finish with the right foot forward, with the body in a sideways hitting position.

Variations include having a player run toward the fence-post at the right rear of the court, and the post at the left rear of the court, as if one were getting in position to play extremely deep balls. Only five or six running steps are necessary in this drill.

All drills can be combined into one routine.

FOREHAND TIPS

1. Start moving to the ball just as the opponent hits the ball.
2. Backswing starts as ball comes off racket strings of the opponent.
3. Hit from a bent knee position.
4. Use an Eastern Forehand grip.
5. Racket back only 180°.
6. Maintain rear foot on playing surface during follow-through.

BACKHAND TIPS

1. Use the Continental or Backhand grip.
2. Allow the free hand to guide the racket head during the back-swing.
3. Ball contact is slightly in front of the forward foot.

4. Keep the racket head above the wrist during ball contact.

5. Stroke through the ball and up during the follow-through.

There are two assumptions for volleying:

VOLLEYING IS EASY

1. Use a Continental grip.

2. Hit from a low bent knee position.

The volley is a ball that is hit before it bounces. It is used as an offensive shot when playing inside the service line. The volleyer can handle the opponent's weak return by volleying the ball deep or at a sharp angle out of reach. This skill is easier to learn than others, because there are fewer variables to consider. You already know how to run, shuffle, change grips and bend to get low. Therefore, it will be easy for you to just *turn, step* and *block*. The slight momentum developed by moving toward the net puts sufficient pace on the ball for beginning play. Ball contact is made in front of the body. The continental or backhand grip is recommended for hitting the volley. The theory is that the player does not need to be concerned about changing grips. Forehand and backhand volleys are made with the same grip. The beginner does not use a backswing in this skill. Using these techniques builds confidence for success at the net. Volleying is easier because court coverage is reduced by moving closer to the net.

This is one aspect of the game that is completely under your control. You toss the ball and you hit it. It is comparable to being allowed the first punch in a prize fight. So plan to win the round, not with a cannon-ball serve, but with good speed and placement. Develop it to be more than the simple act of putting the ball in play.

CONTROL THE SERVE

These are skills that can be practiced at the office, home or just before the match. Observe a tournament match on television to create your own successful image of performing the movement. When practicing indoors however, make sure the chandelier above and the mirror in front of you are covered in your homeowners' policy. The best strategy in learning the serve is to *master the basic motion* before worrying about getting the ball into the proper court.

The continental grip is probably the easiest to use in learning the serve. In singles play, stand as close to the center mark as

Figure 4-7. Feet should be comfortably spaced about shoulder width apart.

possible. This allows you to hit the ball over the lower portion of the net and divides the base line in half so you have less distance to run for the opponent's return. The front foot should point toward the net post when serving to the deuce court and point about six feet further out when serving to the ad court. Feet should be comfortably spaced about shoulder width apart. (See Figure 4-7.) Take a deep breath to get relaxed.

The Backswing and Toss

Begin the serve with the ball in the fingertips of the free hand. Place the ball on the racket throat or strings at waist level (Figure 4-8). The toss is made approximately one foot in front of the baseline and at least as high as the extended reach of the racket (Figure 4-9). The weight is shifted to the back leg and foot as the toss is made (Figure 4-10). This action is to allow transfer of weight and change of momentum to occur in the direction of the opponent (Figure 4-11).

Velocity or service power is developed in three ways.

1. By third class lever action of the racket arm.
2. The speed with which the racket arm moves from the back position.
3. Weight change from back foot to forward position.

This is the same method small players use to develop outstanding serves.

Figure 4-8.

Figure 4-9.

Figure 4-10.

Figure 4-11.

Figure 4-12.

Watching the ball carefully during the toss helps keep the chin up and prevents you from looking at the service court. The momentum developed from the weight change propels the body toward the net, thus causing the hip and shoulder rotation. The racket foot is moved in the same direction and is used to catch and support your weight. Force from the swing is dissipated on the side of the body opposite the racket side. (See Figure 4-12.)

WHAT'S THE SCORE?

Each sport is governed by a specific set of rules. The ITF and USTA established the rules internationally and in the United States. The specific USTA rules are printed in the official appendix. The basic rules are given in this section so the player can quickly adapt to the game with minimum knowledge.

Starting Play

The beginning of a match is more traditionally begun with the "spin of the racket" than by coin toss. Before the spin, one player selects an identifying mark on one side of the racket, but not on the other, or perhaps a trademark on the butt of the racket. One player spins the racket while the other calls the identifying mark. An example might be up or down, or rough or smooth. Winner of the spin has the choice of serving, receiving, or end of the court. When one player elects to serve, the opponent has the choice of side.

Serving the Ball

The server position is behind the baseline and between an imaginary extension of the center mark and the singles sideline. The server puts the ball in play by tossing it in the air with one hand and hitting it with the racket before it touches the ground. The serve is completed after the racket contacts the ball.

The server has two chances to hit the ball in the proper court. When the server makes a bad toss, he is not charged with a fault unless there is a swing and miss. However, a fault is charged when the server steps on the baseline or into the court before the racket contacts the ball. The server hits to alternating receiver courts during the entire game.

Returning the Serve

The position of the receiver should be approximately two to three feet inside the baseline. The beginning server's ball velocity will be limited; therefore, the bounce will be shorter than an intermediate or advanced server's ball. The position should also be in a straight line from the center of the receiver's service court and the server position (see Figure 4-13A, B, C).

Figure 4-13. — A —   — B —   — C —

The ball is in play as the server makes contact and remains in play until the point is decided. After the service, the ball may be hit in flight or after one bounce.

Continuous Play

You Win A Point:

1. When the opponent's ball bounces twice before it is hit.

2. When the opponent volleys the ball before it passes that side of the net.

3. If the opponent catches it or hits it more than once.

4. When the opponent fails to return the ball to your court.

5. If the ball touches the opponent or the opponent's clothing.

Keeping Game Score   Games are won by winning at least four points. A set is won by winning at least six games and a match is won by winning at least two sets. When the game begins, neither player has scored points, therefore, each has a love score. An example of scoring is given below:

Points for the Server	Points for the Receiver	Score
1	0	15-Love
2	0	30-Love
3	0	40-Love
4	0	Game for Server

Each player may win any combination of points. Therefore, a single game might be played for several minutes.

Points for the Server	Points for the Receiver	Score
0	1	Love-15
0	2	Love-30
1	2	15-30
2	2	30-30
3	2	40-30
3	3	40-40 or Deuce
3	4	Advantage Receiver
4	4	Deuce
5	4	Advantage Server
6	4	Server's game

Some beginners incorrectly substitute the score of five to represent fifteen. A game must be won by a two point margin.

One can always be assured of serving to the correct court by observing that:

1. When an even number of points has been played, the serve is made from the deuce court or the right service court. For example, 15–15.

2. When an odd number of points has been played, the service is made from the ad side or the left service court. For example, 15–30.

A set must by won be a margin of two games. Therefore, the score could be any of the following combinations: 6-4; 6-3; 6-2; 6-1 or 6-love. Should the games reach 5-5, play will continue until one player has a two game margin, such as 7- 5. Should the games be tied at 6-6, a tie-breaker may be played. Tie-breakers are generally played when there is a time restriction. The two methods of tie-breakers used are the best 5 of 9 points (9 point tiebreaker) or the best 7 of 12 points (12-point tie-breaker). When either tie-breaker is played the winning player must win by a margin of one game only and would be recorded as 7-6. The most popular (12-point tie-breaker) is given in Figure 4-14. Both are presented in the official rules.

A match is won by completing the best two of three sets. Some special men's tournaments play the best three of five sets.

Set Score

The tie-breaker is a scoring device used to prevent marathon sets and matches.

Normally the tie-breaker goes into effect when the set score reaches 6-all, but at the option of the tournament committee it may take effect at 8-all in one or more complete rounds. Figure 4-14 identifies player position by points.

Set Score

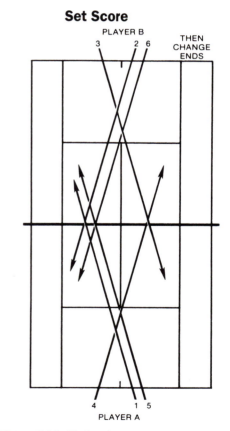

Figure 4-14. Tie-breaker.

Singles   When playing singles, the player who first wins seven points shall win the game and the set, provided the lead is a margin of two points. Should the score reach six points all, the game shall be extended until this 2 point margin has been achieved. Numerical scoring shall be used throughout the tie-breaker.

The player whose turn it is to serve shall be the server for the first point, which is delivered from the right court. The opponent shall be the server for the second and third points (delivered from left court, then right court), and thereafter each player shall serve alternately for two consecutive points (left court, right court) until the winner of the game and set has been decided.

Players shall change ends after every six points and at the conclusion of the tie-breaker. After any change of ends, the server will be serving the second serving point.

Should an error be made in the service order after one point has been played, the point stands and the service order is corrected immediately. If the error is discovered after the second point is in progress the service order remains as altered.

The player who served first in the set that ended in a tie-breaker shall receive service in the first game of the following set or the player who served first in the tiebreaker will receive first in the next set.

Tiebreaker   a. The procedure for singles shall also apply in doubles. Only
for Doubles   the player whose turn it is to serve shall be the server for one point only. Thereafter, each player shall serve in rotation for two points, in the same order as previously in that set, until the winners of the game and set have been decided.

b. Doubles players change ends after every six points and at the conclusion of the tie-breaker.

c. In a doubles tie-breaker when a partner receives out of turn after one point has been played, the point stands and the receiving order is corrected immediately. If the error is recognized after the second point, the receiving order remains as altered.

d. The team that served first in the set that ended in a tie-breaker shall receive service in the first game of the following set, or the player who served first in the tie-breaker will receive first in the next set.

For the short serve drill the player must move to the service line at mid-court and serve two balls over the net from behind right of center service mark to diagonal court. Next, move to left of the center service mark and serve two balls into the opposite court. See Figure 4-15.

Short Serve Drill

Figure 4-15.
The short serve drill.

The machine (or instructor) feeds the ball to the player standing behind the baseline (Figure 4-16). Use two hitters. Four or more students should pick up balls and feed them to the instructor. Special areas can be marked off for a target.

Variations of this drill will improve almost any stroke production.

Ball Machine or Instructor Hitting Drill

Figure 4-16.

The Backboard Can Help

Figure 4-17. Using a backboard.

The backboard can almost duplicate a ball machine. When used *correctly*, it becomes a good friend. It can be used in privacy without distraction. Concentration helps with timing and fluid stroking procedures. The ball returns more quickly from the backboard than from an opponent. Be certain you are controlling the ball, even if it must bounce twice. Experiment with your hitting distance so successful improvement will be apparent. One reason for frustration and poor wall technique is that players pound the ball so wildly, the return "jams" or forces incorrect stroking techniques (Figure 4-17).

Plan your practice to work on one or two movements at a time, such as racket preparation and ball contact. Ask an instructor to demonstrate specific shots and distances for you.

FUN GAMES TO ENHANCE STROKE PROGRESSION

Ball Drop and Weight Transfer

The instructions for the following games are for a right-handed player. Left-handers need to reverse the position. Master each skill before moving to the next progression.

1. Player stands with the left side toward net.

2. Take a short step toward the net with the left foot.

3. Determine that both knees are bent and relaxed. A slight bend at the waist should also be apparent. Body and knees should be mobile to allow for comfortable movement.

4. Drop the ball with the left hand about 14 inches in front of the foot and approximately 6 inches closer to the net. Ball should be dropped so it will bounce up waist high.

5. Perform the ball drop and weight transfer together. Practice several times until it is automatic.

6. Perform the ball drop and catch the ball with the right hand at waist level and continue to swing through the ball so the hand finishes at a point about head high. The catching hand should start from a position perpendicular to the fence behind the court.

7. Practice with a partner. Make constructive remarks to your partner.

8. Try it with a racket. Hold racket by the throat and practice several times. Additional practice should be completed by continually moving the hand down the racket until the hand is placed in the normal grip position.

9. Stand about 20 feet apart. Toss the ball underhanded so it lands at an extended arm racket distance from your partner.

Stroking

Use your own creativity and suggestions from an instructor to practice the backhand drive.

1. Stand in the ready position facing a partner located about 12 feet in front of you.

2. Play catch, tossing underhand to each other. The toss should be below shoulder height and on the throwing side of the player who is catching the ball.

3. Person catching ball should step forward with the left foot and turn the shoulder at the same time. Reach with the right hand to catch the ball. Just prior to catching the ball the weight transfer should be made as the ball is caught on the player's right.

4. Instructor or ball machine feeds a soft ball to the player at the net. Allow 10 hits per player. Two players are set to hit. Four are picking up balls for the instructor

Volley

Player stands about 9 feet away when serving balls into a large net or tennis court fence. Player can make more hits from this position than from the base line on the court.

Service Drill

Name _____

Section _____

Time _____ **Date** _____

Score 1 point for each successful hit.

1. From the base line, drop and hit five balls with the forehand.
    Ball should land behind the opposite service line.   _____ points

2. From the base line drop and hit five balls with the backhand.
    Ball should land behind the opposite service line.   _____ points

3. Hit five consecutive forehands into the singles court without missing.   _____ points

4. Hit five consecutive backhands into the singles court without missing.   _____ points

5. Serve from baseline. Stand in correct service area.
    Serve ten to each court.   _____ points

6. Serve for placement. Each service court is marked in half lengthwise.
    Hit five legal serves to the extreme left of the deuce court then five to
    the right side.   _____ points

7. Stand to the left of center mark. Hit five legal serves to the right of
    the ad court. Then five to the left side.   _____ points

8. Return five of ten serves to singles court.   _____ points

9. Rally twenty-five strokes without missing. Use three separate trials.   _____ points

                                                    TOTAL _____

Your instructor can rate your success.

The Intermediate and Advanced Player

CHAPTER 5

An intermediate player should display knowledge and skill in the following:

1. Name at least 3 changes which have occurred in tennis during the past fifty years.

2. Describe two or more purposes for playing percentage tennis.

3. Describe procedures, and play a 12 point tie breaker.

4. Describe the serve and name at least 10 checkpoints required for a consistently successful serve.

5. Return 25 balls consecutively, that are "set up" to various areas of the court.

6. Describe two styles of singles strategy.

7. Describe and demonstrate 3 drills used for skill improvement

8. Describe and demonstrate two procedures for getting to the net safely.

9. Demonstrate the stroking patterns for the slice and drop shot.

10. Explain the difference between a half-volley and an approach shot.

INTERMEDIATE TENNIS:

EXPECTED ACCOMPLISHMENTS

PRE-TEST — INTERMEDIATE

Name _____   **Date** _____

Section _____   **Time** _____

Before you read any of the material in this section, take the pre-test to determine your tennis knowledge.

Choose the best answer. Place the correct letter in the space provided.

_____ 1. Where should the body weight be located during the follow-through in a forehand drive?

   A. Shifted from the rear to the forward foot
   B. Equally distributed over both feet
   C. Resting primarily on the right foot
   D. Resting primarily on the left foot

_____ 2. Why is the follow-through important in a tennis stroke?

   A. It imparts power to the stroke
   B. It helps assure proper speed and direction
   C. It helps the player to move into position for the next stroke
   D. It is less fatiguing than stroking without a follow-through

_____ 3. Where is the best waiting position during a rally in a singles game?

   A. Near the center of the court and between the service court line and the base line.
   B. Just behind the service court line
   C. Just in front of the service court line
   D. Just behind the center of the base line

_____ 4. Which of the following best describes the type of drive for a baseline player:

   A. Strive for down-the-line shots
   B. Drive the ball so it lands between the service line and the base line
   C. Drive the ball just over the net so that it lands between the service line and the net.
   D. Drive the ball so that it lands deep in bounds, but as far as possible from the opponent

_____ 5. When should the backswing for a stroke be started?

   A. As soon as the ball leaves the opponent's racket
   B. As soon as the ball that is hit by the opponent is across the net
   C. Just as the ball bounces on the hitter's court
   D. As soon as the ball begins to rise from the bounce

_____ 6. In scoring a tennis match, which of the following set of terms is the correct sequence of scoring?

    A. Set, match, game, point
    B. Game, set, point, match
    C. Point, game, set, match
    D. Point, set, game, match

_____ 7. Which of the following situations does not result in a "let" ball?

    A. The serve touches the net and lands in the correct service court
    B. During play, a person from another court interferes with a player's stroke
    C. During the serve, a stray tennis ball hits the receiver as he is executing a backhand stroke
    D. The receiver was not ready for the serve and consequently returned the serve into the net

_____ 8. A ball served underhand strikes the junction of the service line and center line. What is the status of the serve?

    A. The serve is good and ball is in play
    B. The serve is out and should not be played
    C. The serve is a "let" serve and should be played
    D. The serve is a "let" serve and should not be played

_____ 9. A player (while standing outside the tennis court area) returns a ball below net level and outside of the net.

    A. Illegal return, the ball is dead
    B. Legal return, the ball is in play
    C. "Let" the point is played over
    D. "Net," the ball is dead

_____ 10. Which of the following statements best describes the correct method of serving?

    A. The body weight remains distributed equally on both feet throughout the serve. The serving arm is straight when the racket contacts the ball
    B. The body weight is transferred from the rear to the front foot during the serve. The ball is at eye level when contacted by the racket
    C. The body weight is transferred from the rear to the front foot. The serving arm is almost straight when the racket contacts the ball
    D. The body weight remains equal on both feet throughout the serve. The ball is hit when at eye level

_____ 11. Which of the following statements best describes the correct method of volleying the tennis ball when playing the net position?

    A. Wrist bent, punch type of stroke, ball contacted when in line with the body
    B. Wrist bent, full arm swing, ball stroked when in front of the body
    C. Stiff wrist, punch type of stroke, ball contacted in front of the body
    D. Stiff wrist, full arm swing, ball contacted when in line with the body

_____ 12. What is the best strategy to observe when playing doubles?
   A. Both players near the base line
   B. One player near the net, the other player near the base line
   C. Both players parallel to the net, hit most shots to the opponent's alleys
   D. Both players parallel to the net, hit most shots to the middle of the opponent's court

_____ 13. The "side-to-net" position in tennis helps to
   A. Widen the base of support in the direction of the ball
   B. Shorten the distance covered by the racket arm
   C. Take the speed out of the oncoming ball
   D. Shorten the backswing

_____ 14. All of the following statements apply to good tennis sportsmanship
   EXCEPT:
   A. Wait until a point is completed before going to a neighboring court to retrieve a ball
   B. If there is doubt as to whether a ball is good, suggest a replay
   C. If in doubt about the decision of the umpire, question the official rather than your opponent
   D. Figure out your opponent's weaknesses and take advantage of them in your play

_____ 15. The server's score is announced:
   A. Second
   B. First
   C. No pattern in call
   D. Only after every other point

_____ 16. A good drop shot:
   A. Is hit from behind the baseline
   B. Is used against a serve and volleyer
   C. Should bounce six times before it reaches the service line
   D. Is difficult to hit

_____ 17. The racket which provides the most power for the player is:
   A. A highly crafted wood frame
   B. One of those new wide-bodies
   C. Any standard size frame
   D. One that is strung with gut

_____ 18. Which of the following is a defensive measure against a net player?
   A. A hard drive
   B. A volley
   C. A trick shot
   D. A lob

_____ 19. Topspin is effective for most players because:
  A. The ball will land deeper in the opponent's court
  B. The ball can be hit harder with less likelihood of it going out
  C. It usually clears the net more easily
  D. All of the above

_____ 20. Practice serves are taken:
  A. Before normal warm-up with your opponent
  B. Just before you serve the first point of a match
  C. Any time during the match
  D. At the beginning of each set

_____ 21. What happens when doubles partners line up incorrectly and play a point?
  A. The team that incures the error loses the point
  B. The point is replayed
  C. The point stands and correction is made immediately
  D. The line up remains, but is changed at the end of the game

_____ 22. Which of the following tournaments represent the "Grand Slam" of tennis?
  A. U.S. Open, Italian, Wimbledon, Australian
  B. Australian, French, Wimbledon, U.S. Open
  C. Australian, French, German, U.S. Open
  D. Australian, Davis Cup, Wimbledon, U.S. Open

_____ 23. The correct score in a regulation match would be:
  A. 6-4, 2-5
  B. 7-6, 6-6, 7-6
  C. 2-6, 6-5
  D. 6-3, 1-6, 6-4

_____ 24. Which of the following statements is correct for a player who swings at a lob that hits in the court and misses?
  A. Player may swing again
  B. Point is played over
  C. Player loses the point
  D. None of the above

_____ 25. Your first serve hits your partner playing the net position.
  A. Play the serve over
  B. Count it as a fault
  C. Play a let
  D. Let your partner serve

Name _____

Section _____

Time _____ Date _____

Form Analysis Chart

	Observation #1	Observation #2	Evaluation	
				Place the appropriate number in the space provided for the specific skill or movement.

Professional or near perfect　_5_

Outstanding　_4_

Average　_3_

Needs Improving　_2_

Poor　_1_

SERVE

Correct grip ....

Comfortable stance ....

Toe pointed correctly ....

Accurate toss ....

Chin up ....

Adequate weight change ....

Rhythmic backswing ....

Full backswing ....

Racket arm extended at impact ....

Hitting up and out ....

Follow-through ....

Backfoot across the baseline ....

Ball control ....

FOREHAND

Eastern forehand ....

Return to ready position ....

Racket preparation ....

Correct footwork ....

Swing ....

Ball contact ....

Weight transfer ....

Follow-through ....

Ball control ....

Add the totals and observe the chart below to categorize your form.

Professional or near perfect	175-190 points
Advanced amateur or more successes than errors	150-174 points
Hacker or more errors than successes	100-124 points
Inept or many more errors than successes	75-99 points

(Continued)

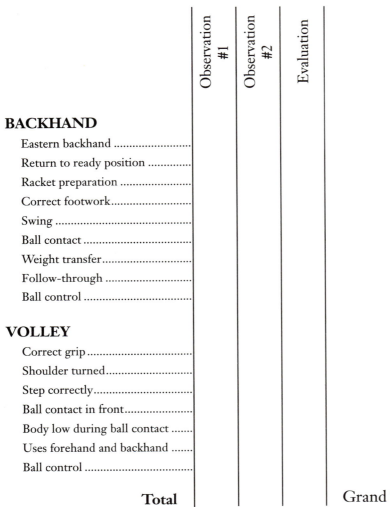

	Observation #1	Observation #2	Evaluation
BACKHAND			
Eastern backhand			
Return to ready position			
Racket preparation			
Correct footwork			
Swing			
Ball contact			
Weight transfer			
Follow-through			
Ball control			
VOLLEY			
Correct grip			
Shoulder turned			
Step correctly			
Ball contact in front			
Body low during ball contact			
Uses forehand and backhand			
Ball control			
Total			

Grand Total Evaluation _____

To improve technique, read sections relating to specific skills.

An advanced player will, at the beginning of instruction, display skill and knowledge greater than that of an intermediate player.

The advanced player should be able to:

1. Exhibit a knowledge of 90% of the terms in the glossary.

2. Describe two problems associated with each of the following: tennis elbow, equipment selection and the Western forehand.

3. Demonstrate and describe two drills each for the serve, volley and groundstroke.

4. Sustain a rally of 40 legal hits which land within eight feet of the baseline. The balls should not exceed a height of six feet above the net.

5. Sustain a volley of ten legal hits that simulate playing conditions.

6. List two reasons for joining the USTA.

7. Successfully describe the difference between a defensive lob and offensive lob.

8. Describe the selection of four items of tennis equipment.

9. Explain the procedure for hitting an overhead smash.

10. List three different serves and a value for each type.

ADVANCED TENNIS:

EXPECTED ACCOMPLISHMENTS

PRE-TEST — ADVANCED

Name _____ **Date** _____

Section _____ **Time** _____

Before you read any of the material in this section, take the pre-test to determine your tennis knowledge.

Choose the best answer. Place the correct letter in the space provided.

_____ 1. In serving, why is it important to toss the ball high enough that it can be hit with the serving arm fully extended?
- A. This enables the server to serve with a more natural swing than would otherwise be possible
- B. This enables the server to use the entire body as a lever, thus getting more power behind the ball
- C. This gives the server ample time to correctly time the serve
- D. This assures the server of greater accuracy in placing the serve

_____ 2. When contacting the ball on the serve, where should the body weight be located for a right-handed server?
- A. Over the right foot
- B. Over the left foot
- C. Equally over both feet
- D. Weight transfers from the rear to the forward foot

_____ 3. What should a player do when stroking a low bouncing ball?
- A. Drop the racket head and scoop upward on the ball
- B. Bend from the waist, keeping the racket face parallel to the net
- C. Chip or slice the ball
- D. Go for a winner

_____ 4. How many sets constitute a match in men's play?
- A. Two out of three sets
- B. Three out of five sets
- C. Four out of seven sets
- D. None of the above are correct

_____ 5. How does the volley differ from the drive?
- A. The volley is used to "put the ball away"
- B. The volley is a defensive shot used to gain time
- C. The volley requires a longer follow-through than does the drive
- D. Recommended foot placement differs

_____   6.   Which strategy is more effective in singles play?
        A.   Repeated driving down the line
        B.   Volleying
        C.   Lobbing
        D.   Varying placements and pace

_____   7.   Which of the statements below best describes body position at contact with ball during a backhand drive?
        A.   Bent arm, facing the net, contact the ball when it is forward of the body toward the net
        B.   Bent arm, sideways to the net, contact the ball when it is forward of the body toward the net
        C.   Straight arm, facing the net, contact the ball when it is forward of the body toward the net
        D.   Bent arm, sideways to the net, contact the ball when it is even with the body

_____   8.   The high-lob shot is generally used for which of the following reasons?
        A.   To force an opponent to vacate the net position
        B.   To enable one to have time to get into the correct playing position
        C.   To put a lot of spin ("English") on the tennis ball and make an opponent look into the sun
        D.   Both A and B above

_____   9.   Which of the following descriptions best applies to returning a high lob?
        A.   Aim your return at the opponent's feet, attempt to use the back hand smash whenever possible
        B.   Hit the ball while it is still high in the air. Place the ball close to the net on the opponent's court
        C.   Hit toward the opponent's feet, place a lot of spin on the ball
        D.   Stroke the ball as in serving, hit deep, away from the opponent

_____   10.   During which phase of the bounce is it best to stroke the ball when returning a serve?
        A.   When the ball is falling toward the ground
        B.   When it is rising from the surface
        C.   Top part of the bounce
        D.   All phases of the bounce

_____   11.   Which of the following is considered the best strategy to observe when playing a tennis match?
        A.   Play the opponent's weakness
        B.   Drive all balls to the opponent's backhand
        C.   Drive all balls to the opponent's base line
        D.   Run the opponent as much as possible

_____ 12. A smash in tennis is **BEST** described as a
- A. Stroke used to strike the ball at its highest point in flight
- B. Stroke made by hitting the ball before it has touched the ground
- C. Fast over-head stroke intended to put the ball away before it has touched the ground
- D. Ball that is hit high into the air

_____ 13. All of the following associations concerning a tennis tournament are correct **EXCEPT**:
- A. Elimination tournament — if one match is lost, the player is dropped
- B. Ladder tournament — the play starts with the players at the bottom of the scale and continues upward until the grand winner is determined
- C. Round robin tournament — the player competes against every participant in the tournament
- D. Handicap tournament — the more advanced player gives the weaker player at least one point on each game

_____ 14. The court should lie north and south because of
- A. Wind
- B. Sun rays
- C. Tempertive transition
- D. Tradition

_____ 15. The best fundamental for the average player is:
- A. Strive for accuracy
- B. Strive for speed
- C. Keep weight on back foot
- D. Keep body front facing the net

_____ 16. What happens in a doubles match when a player returns a ball that passes outside the net post below the level of the top of the net and hits in the opponent's court.
- A. Its a dead ball
- B. Player who hits the shot loses the point
- C. Player who hits the shot wins the point
- D. Play a let

_____ 17. Which statement is false?
- A. A server may drop the ball and serve it from the bounce
- B. The player may serve underhanded
- C. The server makes the toss, then catches it
- D. The server may bounce the ball and catch it

_____ 18. A base line player hitting off the back foot will result in:
- A. Reduced power
- B. Additional power
- C. More accurate placement
- D. Foot problems

_____ 19. A two-handed shot is:

    A. More effective than a one-handed
    B. Used by weaker players
    C. One that has few disadvantages
    D. Used by players at all levels

_____ 20. When playing on slow courts:

    A. Serve and volley
    B. End the points quickly
    C. Go for Winners
    D. Play a base line game

_____ 21. Most tennis professional's service toss:

    A. Is hit on the way up
    B. Is hit at the peak of toss
    C. Is 6 to 12 inches higher than the extended reach
    D. Is just above the head

_____ 22. A player loses the point, if during the point:

    A. He/she touches the net with the racket
    B. He/she touches the net with the foot
    C. Touches the net with clothing
    D. All of the above

_____ 23. In doubles, a ball hit through the middle of the court should be returned by which player:

    A. Best player should return the ball
    B. Player with the best forehand
    C. The quickest player to the ball
    D. The player whose turn it is

_____ 24. Before the return of serve during doubles, the netperson on the receiving team should stand:

    A. At the base line
    B. Close to the net
    C. On the service line
    D. Anywhere in the backcourt

_____ 25. Before the serve in doubles the netperson on the service side should be positioned:

    A. In the alley about 6 feet from the net
    B. On the baseline
    C. Anywhere in the backcourt
    D. About 8 feet from the net

Name _____

Section _____

Time _____ Date _____

Form Analysis Chart

	Observation #1	Observation #2	Evaluation

Place the appropriate number in the space provided for the specific skill or movement.

Professional or near perfect   <u>5</u>

Outstanding   <u>4</u>

Average   <u>3</u>

Needs Improving   <u>2</u>

Poor   <u>1</u>

SERVE

Correct grip.............................

Comfortable stance ....

Toe pointed correctly ....

Accurate toss...........................

Chin up.................................

Adequate weight change...............

Rhythmic backswing ....

Full backswing ....

Racket arm extended at impact ....

Hitting up and out......................

Follow-through ....

Backfoot across the baseline.........

Ball control ....

FOREHAND

Eastern forehand ....

Return to ready position ....

Racket preparation ....

Correct footwork............ ....

Swing ....

Ball contact ....

Weight transfer...........................

Follow-through ....

Ball control ....

Add the totals and observe the chart below to categorize your form.

Professional or near perfect	175-190 points
Advanced amateur or more successes than errors	150-174 points
Hacker or more errors than successes	100-124 points
Inept or many more errors than successes	75-99 points

(Continued)

	Observation #1	Observation #2	Evaluation
BACKHAND			
Eastern backhand			
Return to ready position			
Racket preparation			
Correct footwork			
Swing			
Ball contact			
Weight transfer			
Follow-through			
Ball control			
VOLLEY			
Correct grip			
Shoulder turned			
Step correctly			
Ball contact in front			
Body low during ball contact			
Uses forehand and backhand			
Ball control			
Total			

Grand Total Evaluation _____

To improve technique, read sections relating to specific skills.

The Forehand Shot may be the most frequently hit shot in a match (Figure 5-1). The Eastern grip is taught by most professionals. However, many players have been successful with the Continental and the semi-Western grip.

THE FOREHAND

—A —   —B —

—C —   —D —

Figure 5-1. The Forehand Shot.

Some players begin the backswing just as they realize the ball is coming over the net to the forehand side. We recommend that you start the backswing as the ball leaves the strings of the opponent's racket. The real key is to allow enough time to adjust to spin or the speed of the ball. The backswing is usually a straight, flat swing that moves behind the body 180° from the net. The body is turned sideways from the net or at a right angle. The lead shoulder would be perpendicular to the net. As one progresses in skill, a circular backswing or loop may be effective. The purpose is to develop a smooth, fluid swing.

Ball contact for a player with an Eastern grip would be about even or ahead of the lead foot. The player with a Western grip would make contact slightly earlier. Those using the Continental grip would make contact later than the previous two.

When possible, make contact with the ball waist high and make the follow-through a little higher than the shoulder.

Forehand Tips

1. Start moving to the ball just as the opponent hits the ball.
2. The backswing starts as ball comes off racket strings of the opponent.
3. Hit from a bent knee position.
4. Use an Eastern Forehand grip.

Corrective Techniques for Forehand Errors

Error:	Player hits the ball off the back foot.
Correction:	Use early racket preparation. Bring racket back as ball leaves opponent's strings.
Error:	Player stands facing the net, hits hard, but seems to have little power.
Correction:	Player is not turning so he/she should step toward the net and make ball contact in front of and to the side of the leading foot.
Error:	Player is miss-hitting the ball.
Correction:	Back swing may be way over 200°. This changes the shoulder alignment. The ball is hit later, thus reducing ability to see the ball properly. Use only 180° backswing so the line of vision is never lost.

5. Racket back only 180°.

6. Maintain rear foot on playing surface during follow-through.

THE BACKHAND

A well-executed backhand begins with the player pivoting sideways to the ball (Figure 5-2). The grip will have changed to the Continental or backhand discussed earlier. The racket can be guided to the backswing by allowing the free hand to rest under the throat.

As with the forehand, the backswing will begin early. Attempt to time ball contact at about waist high. The ball contact occurs earlier with the backhand drive than with the forehand drive. Ball contact can be made a few inches in front of the lead foot. To avoid using wrist action, imagine the wrist and arm in a cast to just above the elbow. With a high follow-through, the ball will go over the net with topspin. With a level follow-through, it will stay at the same height. A low follow-through will put the ball into the net.

To hit the backhand with underspin, the racket is brought back high, then the swing is down on the ball in a "cutting" motion. Just close the racket face slightly and reduce the follow-through.

—A—   —B—   — C —

Figure 5-2. The Backhand Shot.

Backhand Tips
1. Use the Continental or backhand grip.
2. Bring the racket back early Start the backswing as the ball leaves the opponent's strings.
3. Place the free hand under the throat to keep the racket head up during the backswing.
4. Make ball contact slightly in front of and to the side of the forward foot.
5. To hit a topspin drive, allow the follow-through to continue out toward the opponent and up above the racket arm shoulder.

Corrective Techniques for Backhand Errors

Error:	Contacting the ball late.
Correction:	Contact ball in front of and to the side of the leading foot.
Error:	Trajectory is low. Grip may be incorrect.
Correction:	Use Continental grip. Use a complete follow-through.
Error:	Trajectory is high.
Correction:	Mentally place wrist and arm in a cast to prevent wrist movement. Avoid opening up the racket face.

THE TWO-HANDED PLAYER

Jimmy Conners, Christ Evert, Cliff Drysdale, and a host of others have used two hands very successfully.

With the two-handed backhand the Eastern grip is used with both hands. The left hand is on the top and the right hand is at the bottom. The backswing is usually lower and closer to the body. At ball contact the swing is for topspin. The follow-through is slightly shorter than if one hand were used. This is easy for young children and others who do not believe they are strong enough. As a result, more power is generated.

Most two-handed players experience more difficulty volleying and do not have the reach during baseline play that one-handers have. It is also difficult to change the pace with a slice return. If you decide to use the two-handed grip, develop quickness in footwork and learn to anticipate.

The approach shot is a groundstroke used on a short ball at mid-court and followed to the net. One anticipates forcing a weak volley or lob, then winning the point with a crosscourt volley or overhead shot (Figure 5-3).

The safest method of getting to the net is to hit a good approach shot. Because the shot is played off a short ball, the backswing used to hit the approach is shorter than the standard groundstroke, otherwise the ball is hit long or into the net. Or when playing against a two-handed backhand player, a good strategy is to slice the approach shot far enough away from the opponent to make him/her take one hand off the racket. This reduces the power and accuracy for the two-handed player. Unfortunately, some intermediates move back to the base line after the approach, and get caught retreating.

Go for the shot when the ball bounces at least as high as the net near your service line and close to the center of the court. When the ball is lower, it is more difficult to control.

The best place to hit the shot is deep to the opponent's weak side or deep down the line. Any approach should be hit with more slice than the standard groundstroke.

THE APPROACH SHOT

—A— —B— —C—

Figure 5-3.

VOLLEY TO WIN The successful volleyer gets ready to move quickly in any direction, and a low position is necessary for ball control. The principle movement is made when your front shoulder turns toward the ball. The power is generated on this stroke by the forward movement of your body. Visualize your wrist and arm in a cast moving from the shoulder to the ball. Once the *turn*, *step* and *block* technique have been mastered, the more advanced player can take a short backswing to provide additional punch. When possible, the racket head, your eyes, and the ball should be on the same level at impact.

Anticipate early by realizing your opponent will attempt a percentage return. This should help you cut off the angle, and it may force the opponent to hit a lower percentage shot. Avoid laying the racket back.

Occasionally, you may hit a volley from a deep position because you were caught out of position. This volley should be hit deep into the opponent's court to allow time for your recovery and your return to a central position.

Most of your volleys will occur between the service line and within 8–10 feet of the net. If you move too close, the opponent is set for the easy lob. See Figure 5-4.

Figure 5-4.

Figure 5-5. Normal volley.

Figure 5-6. Drop volley.

Figure 5-7. High volley.

Figure 5-8. Low volley.

Tips for the Volley   1. Think in terms of little or no backswing.

2. Attempt to hit the ball at eye level.

3. Always attack. Hit the ball in front of the body. This automatically keeps elbows away from the body.

4. Arm and racket should move from the shoulder. Remember to visualize the wrist and arm in a cast.

5. When possible, keep the racket head above the wrist. This produces almost perfect control.

6. Use a firm grip at impact.

7. Attempt to have forward movement with ball impact.

8. Should you not win the point, be ready for the next.

9. Before hitting a volley keep the free hand on the throat of the racket.

Corrective Techniques for the Volley

Error:	The player continually miss-hits or misses completely.
Correction:	Instruct player to move within two-three feet of the net and make contact with the ball before it passes over the net.
Error:	The player swings at a volley as he/she has been taught for a ground stroke.
Correction:	The instructor or another player can stand to the side of the volleyer. This prompts the forward step and should eliminate the backswing.
Error:	The player drops the racket head to the knees when volleying.
Correction:	The player has probably let the ball come to him/her. Player should stay low, move forward and attempt to hit the ball at eye level.

As noted earlier, the player serving can control the match with a properly executed serve (Figure 5-9).

Most top amateurs and professionals use one of the tosses listed below.

1. Hit the ball on the way up.

2. Hit at the height of the toss. The ball is at a dead position at the top of the peak. It is suspended momentarily in the air.

3. Toss twelve or more inches above full racket extension. This extra height allows for more adjustments at the last moment.

The problem most of us develop is tossing it too low. When this happens, the accuracy and power are changed significantly. Full arm extension must be maintained during ball contact.

The Continental or modified backhand grip should be used by advanced players. Ball spin and control are more easily developed using this grip.

Ball contact happens as though the racket is hitting up on the ball. The ball cannot travel in a straight line from point of racket contact and land in the service court. It will hit the net first.

SUCCESSFUL TECHNIQUES FOR THE SERVE

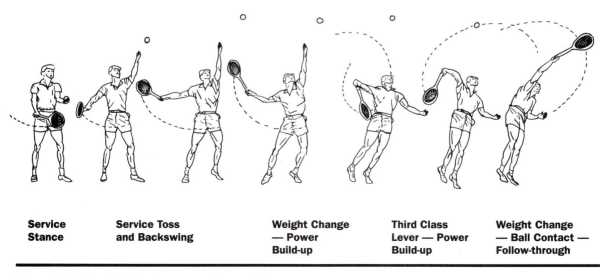

| Service Stance | Service Toss and Backswing | Weight Change — Power Build-up | Third Class Lever — Power Build-up | Weight Change — Ball Contact — Follow-through |

Figure 5-9. Steps to follow for a properly-executed serve.

Just visualize the arc from which the racket will swing in this third class lever position. The lift begins at shoulder level and the body flows upward as the racket moves through the hitting area. The body extends for a powerful hit. The larger the arc, the more effective the swing. Therefore, the serve is more effective.

The Flat, Slice and Spin Serves

Three different serves are used by the advanced player. The flat serve is hit just above and to the side of the very center of the ball. (A ball hit directly in the center by a six foot player will hit the net or be long.) This serve is sometimes referred to as the cannonball and is difficult to control.

The slice is hit at about one or two o'clock for a right-handed player. It has a deceptive bounce because of the sidespin. It bounces away from a right-handed player's forehand or spins into the body. This serve is used as the second serve.

The American twist or top spin is the most difficult to use. The ball is hit by a right-hander between ten and twelve o'clock. The serve can be hit by as much as eight feet over the net and drop in the court with severe top spin. It is a high percentage serve, but slower than the other two mentioned.

A Recap on Serving

1. Correct grip.

2. Feet comfortably placed. Front foot should be angled toward net post.

3. Address your opponent. Ball is on fingertips and placed at the throat or on strings of racket. Racket head up toward opponent.

4. Toss with the fingers. Release about head high.

5. Toss will rise above full extension of extended racket arm. Toss inside the base line or in front of your body.

6. Above movements should help keep chin up.

7. Weight moves to the back foot on toss, to the front foot at ball impact. Weight then moves up and out toward the opponent.

8. The backswing should be rhythmic or one continuous movement.

9. Backswing should be to the full "backscratch" position for the third class lever action to occur. The butt of the racket should point to the sky.

10. Racket arm extended. If it is not fully extended, the third class lever arm is shortened and power is reduced.

11. Hit up and out as though you're hitting toward the sky.

12. The follow-through is a continuous motion in the direction of the hit. The energy and weight transfer moves the body into the court as a part of the follow- through. The energy is dissipated during the follow-through on the opposite side of the body.

Corrective Techniques for the Serve:

Error: Serve is long.

Correction: Move the toss out further or in the direction of the error. Check your grip. You may need to reduce ball speed.

Error: Serve into the net.

Correction: Serve is too far into the court. Toss closer to base line. Move toss in the direction of the error.

Error: No power.

Correction: Check your stance. Increase standing angle away from net. Toss must also be high enough that full extension occurs. Serve is a third class lever action. Racket arm speed is also a vital function.

Error: Loss of power and accuracy.

Correction: Finish the follow-through after making ball contact. Some players stop the swing within a foot or so after ball contact. You have generated power with; 1) third class lever function, 2) speed from the movement, 3) weight transfer, and 4) body rotation. Yet, the swing is stopped almost immediately after contact. A large number of antagonistic muscles were brought into play long before ball contact. It's like having the brakes on while accelerating your 560 SL. Practice the complete serve routine emphasizing the follow-through.

Return the Serve Consistently

The primary objective of the service return is to *get it back*. Do not try for a winner. The idea is to protect the point. The service return is the second most important shot in the game, and most players never practice returning service.

Place an imaginary dot in the center of the serving box, then draw an imaginary line from the server, through the dot to your receiving position. The primary key is to get the ball as quickly as possible. This should position you so that you do not have to take more than one step to return the ball.

Get up on your toes so you can move forward on the serve. However, the quick jumping movement which is characteristic of many highly advanced players is unnecessary. They are trying to be as "light on the feet" as possible so an easy pivot can be made. Simply attempt to move in against the serve rather than back up.

Many served balls will bounce high. Therefore, your body position should also be high when ball contact is made.

Hit the ball on the rise. This may necessitate moving inside the base line on balls with severe top spin. Otherwise, ball contact would be above shoulder level.

Hit the return with a firm wrist and short backswing. The velocity of the returned ball and your forward momentum will provide sufficient power. Because you have less time for racket preparation, a blocking motion is used. This chip shot should be returned deep and on the same line of flight that it came to you.

DROP SHOT

The drop shot is a gingerly hit shot that requires touch control and timing (Figure 5-10). It is used to pull a player from the baseline into the net, to change the rhythm and to tire the opponent. A good drop shot will bounce six times before it gets to the service line.

The Continental (or volley grip) provides an open-faced racket for underspin. It is an offensive shot hit by a player that is well inside the base line. Normal stroke preparation is used when

Figure 5-10. —A—   —B—

executing the drop shot. This aids in the deception. Relax the wrist and swing from high to low to high.

The lob has no charm or charisma. Perhaps that is the reason few instructors teach it. But it is **the** tennis stroke that can get you out of a hole and equalize the match (see Figure 5-11). The only difference between the lob and a drive is the angle of ball ascent.

THE LOB

—A—

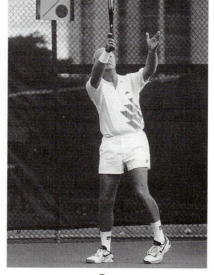

—B—

—C—

—D—

Figure 5-11. Proper technique for hitting a lob.

The degree of turn of the racket face is the primary difference in the two strokes. The speed of the stroke, and the low backswing to a high follow-through adds to the proficiency of success. A high defensive lob should clear the net by twenty-five to thirty feet and bounce within six-eight feet of the base line. Any lob falling inside the service line allows the opponent to hit the smash from the air.

Move into position as you would to hit any ground stroke. One purpose is to surprise the opponent, to catch him/her moving to the net. The weight is shifted forward as in a standard drive, but the follow-through is shorter. The defensive underspin results from the open face of the racket. On a backhand lob the racket head is low to high.

The top spin offensive lob is a very advanced shot which requires perfect conditions and perfect timing. The ball moves in about the same trajectory as a low lob, but has terrific top spin which causes it to drop rapidly after it reaches a high peak and then it bounces low and fast toward the fence. The purpose is to get the ball to peak above the opponent's head. If it peaks earlier, it is usually a smash for the opponent. When it peaks late, it may go out. This is a low percentage shot used only when you're in control of the game.

THE OVERHEAD SMASH

The overhead smash requires more patience than other strokes, because it seems so easy. Most players run up to "cream" the ball and hit either the fence or the net. We encourage players to reduce power about 50 percent. This philosophy tends to keep the player cool. More concentration can be placed on accuracy and depth rather than power (Figure 5-12).

The overhead is patterned after the service motion. The difference is in using a modified back swing.

1. Use the same grip that is used on the serve.
2. Take long steps to get to the area, then short quick steps to get in position.
3. Turn your side to the net.
4. Position yourself under the ball. Swing upward and forward to meet the ball in line with the racket shoulder. This helps reduce panic in the remainder of the stroke.
5. Track the ball with the index finger on the non-racket hand. This helps in turning and provides better perception while following the ball on its descent.

—A—   —B—   **Figure 5-12.** Overhead smash.

6. Make contact as high as possible and slightly in front of the body. If the ball gets behind you or you hit it too soon, it will be too long. If it is too far in front or drops too low, it will hit the net.

7. Follow through. Hit out and down. Otherwise, the racket head drags down too sharply and the ball hits into the net.

8. Allow a deep lob to bounce. Just make sure you make contact before it drops too low after the bounce.

SINGLES STRATEGY

Competition is the basis of tennis and stimulates the player into improving his/her game. To compete well requires some planning and goal setting. Those who have played tournament tennis realize there is no perfect strategy for singles. Amateur and professionals often change plans between sets. The basic style played is probably a serve and volley game, a base line game, or an all court game.

Whatever the style, high percentage tennis is vital to consistent winning. Any mistakes made should be those of the opponent. High accuracy percentages develop into reality by utilizing the techniques taught earlier in the text. Patience, tenacity and hitting deep down the middle prevents many problems. Determine that you will play a marathon match! Keep the point alive. Don't blow it.

The net game will be used by most advanced players that have learned to hit the approach shot and volley consistently. This constant pressure will force the opponent to make numerous errors.

The player that waits to see how short a ball hits probably will spend too much time thinking and will be pulled out of position. This sort of indecision will wreck one's game.

To play percentage tennis from the baseline requires three automatic responses:

1. Get to the ball quickly.

2. Prepare racket early (backswing begins as the ball leaves the opponent's strings).

3. Hit the ball at least three feet over the net (Figure 5-13).

These actions increase the probability of keeping the ball in play because:

▶ It reduces your margin of error.

▶ It keeps the opponent deep and prevents an attacking game.

▶ The ball stays in the air longer. This allows time for your recovery and return to the basic position.

The margin of error is further reduced by hitting above the center of the net because it is six inches lower at the center. The singles court is four feet, six inches longer on the diagonal than down the line. This greater space also reduces the margin of error when the ball is hit cross court.

As one moves from the base line toward the net, the angle of percentage increases with each step (Figure 5-14). Down the line shot possibilities are much greater inside the service line than from the base line position. This net play often moves the opponent away from the strong percentage shot. Overplay the

Figure 5-13. Hit the ball at least three feet over the net.

Figure 5-14. Bisect the angle.

strength. Tempt your opponent into hitting what appears to be an easy shot. This tactic also assists you in maintaining control of the game.

The player that has not reached the advanced skill and condition level will stay at the base line. Rely on the "bread and butter shots." Don't throw caution to the wind.

Control the game by forcing the opponent to hit the shot you want him/her to hit. When he/she expects a hard hitting rhythmic game, slow it down, dink it, lob it , and change the pace to upset the momentum. A player whose timing is thrown off, often blows the game.

Learn to bisect the angle. This involves the strategic position of your play as well as the opponent's. The large space or large angle is the safe space to hit.

The following strategies should be considered by the singles player:

▶ Establish your game plan on the basis of your playing strength.

▶ Recognize the ability of your opponent.

▶ Determine to move forward toward the service line, not back.

▶ Hit deep to keep your opponent at the base line.

▶ Every shot is important because it may be your last.

▶ When the opponent sends you wide to either side of the court, hit the lob to change your opponent's rhythm. This allows you to recover and return to a basic position.

RECREATIONAL DOUBLES

The club player will often find the up and back position or both players at the base line to be more pleasant, because play is much slower. Reactions don't have to be as quick.

The serve and net play of both players may be weak, therefore base line play is more comfortable. Neither feel they are going to get killed at the net.

When playing recreationally, the following characteristics should be apparent.

1. Don't poach unless you feel very confident of the point.

2. Hit away from the net player.

3. Keep the ball deep on the serve and place it to the weak sides on lobs.

4. Be sure to switch sides on lobs.

5. Keep the ball in play.

DOUBLES: BE SMART LIKE THE PROFESSIONAL

Who Serves First?

The stronger partner should serve first. He will serve twice in the first six games. The weaker partner will serve once. For example, Chris is the strong server on her team and serves first and wins. Karen's team starts with its weak server who loses serve. The score is 2-0 as Chris's partner serves. Assuming she loses and Karen's team wins its serve, the score is 2-2. Karen's team will lose the set if the same routine continues for the next four games. The score is 4-4, then Karen's weaker server is up again. If she is broken and Chris holds the serve, the set is over and the score is 6-4.

Often the sun can be a significant factor. It is probably wise to let a left hander serve from the end which looks away from the sun. This will allow the right hander to look away from it at the opposite end.

Remember, your team does not have to serve first. You may realize the opponents are slow starters. This allows a golden opportunity of breaking serve early.

The competent team which moves to the net with offensive tactics will control the match. Those with weak strokes will experience problems at the net.

The player serving or receiving will move to the net as quickly as possible. This support given to your net partner tends to intimidate the opponents. The key is to make sure both are at the net together on offense or together at the base line on defense. A distance of 10-12 feet between players is recommended. The one up and one back position is only for recreational players and those who want to lose.

The player closest to the net has the responsibility on all shots within reach. Each player is responsible for any ball that goes over the head, from the net to the base line.

The majority of points won during a rally will be won by hitting down the middle. The net is lower at the center and you reduce the angle of return. It also creates indecision for the opponents when hit down the middle.

The indecision can be partially eliminated by deciding before hand that one partner will cover slightly more than half of the court. This tactic also helps force the opponents to the lower percentage alley shots.

When playing advanced doubles, the left-handed player is often on the right side so both players will be playing the forehand down the middle.

Talk to each other. But make only positive remarks. Wait until the end of the match to offer constructive criticism. If your partner believes he is performing poorly, his entire game will fall apart.

The winning team will be the one that overcomes the obstacles presented by the opponent.

Gain Quick Momentum by Working Together

Stand in the middle of the service court (Figure 5-15.). This pressures the receiver into hitting a good cross court return. It also makes the low percentage alley a more inviting area for the return.

Poach at every opportunity. Poaching means to cross over into the server's half of the court to volley the service return. Coordinate your efforts by establishing signals for poaching. Signals can be used with the hand, the racket or a clenched fist. I have used the clenched fist to indicate that Bob better not get me killed with that forty MPH serve of his.

Where Do I Stand When My Partner Is Serving?

Figure 5-15. The correct position on the court when your partner is serving.

The net player on the serving team should be thinking, "I'm hitting the next ball", "you can't get it by me." Many of those we observe appear to be thinking, "I hope it's not hit to me." "Hit it to him!" The opponent quickly senses the fear of this lethargic player and hits most of the balls to this "muffer." Alert, positive action will make a difference in team momentum.

Where Do I Stand When My Partner is Receiving?

Stand at the middle of the service line or within one-half step of the line. This allows the player to be in a position which protects the middle of the court. This position reduces the opponent's angle when following the service return.

Just keep in mind, the entire net position is the responsibility of the net player.

The Service Return in Doubles

This is probably the second most important shot in doubles. The major purpose is to keep the ball in play. This can be accomplished by keeping the ball away from the net player. Hit at the feet of the attacking server.

You eliminate problems by assuming all returns are to be hit cross court. The time to consider hitting down the line is when the net player is poaching on most of the serves.

Any team that forces the opponent to hit up on the ball will allow you to hit down and control the game.

Generally, the better player or left-hander will receive in the ad court. In the deuce court, the right-hander can return most serves on the forehand side.

If the server is "smokin' em" by you, move back more. If it is a spin serve, move up and hit it on the rise.

CHAPTER 6

Drills and Skill Tests

DRILLS TO BUILD CONFIDENCE

Drill

1. **A** serves 10 balls to one corner, then 10 balls to the other corner.
2. **B** returns the balls to one of the two corners marked.

ONE-ON-ONE: CROSS COURT SHOT, FOREHAND TO FOREHAND AND BACKHAND TO BACKHAND

Drill

1. Players are to keep the ball in play and deep.
2. Each player should hit 10 consecutive balls to complete the drill.

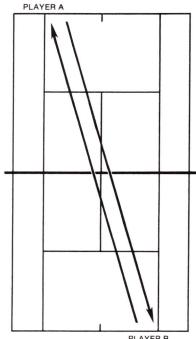

Figure 6-1. One-on-One.

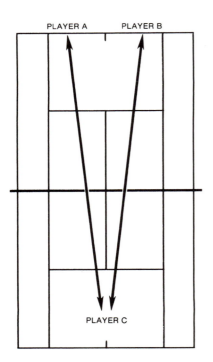

TWO-ON-ONE: LOBS AND OVERHEAD SMASH

Purpose

1. To teach players to use defensive lobs.
2. Teach players to position correctly when hitting the smash.

Drill

1. Player **A** and **B** hit lobs to player **C**.
2. Player **C** hits the smash using only 50% power. Accuracy is the key.
3. Players change positions when **C** hits successful smashes.

Figure 6-2. Lobs and Overhead Smash.

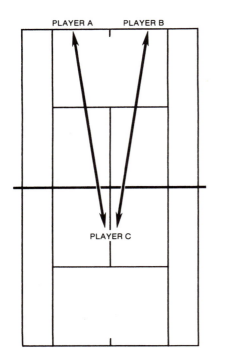

TWO-ON-ONE: VOLLEYS

Purpose

To teach volleyers to react quickly to hard drives.

Drill

1. Players **A** and **B** hit hard drives to volleyer.
2. Player **C** practices forehand and backhand volley. Concentrate on form

Figure 6-3. Volleys.

TWO-ON-ONE: FOREHAND AND BACKHAND GROUNDSTROKES

Purpose

1. To teach players instinctive moves toward correct position for baseline strokes.
2. Hit three feet over the net.
3. Hit deep within two feet of the baseline.
4. Return to the ready position.

Drill

1. Player **A** and **B** alternate hitting the ball to player **C** which moves **C** first to the forehand then to the backhand.
2. This drill can be varied by adding another player. The players move to the alley behind the base line. Each player should hit a minimum of 10 forehands and 10 backhands into the alley before concluding the drill.

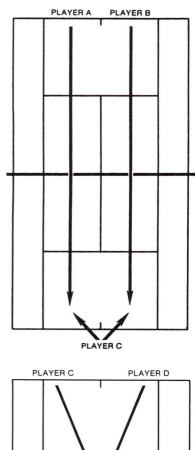

Figure 6-4. Forehand and Backhand Ground Strokes.

SERVE: FOUR ON FOUR

Purpose

To improve server's aim to designated area in forehand and backhand corners.

Drill

1. Each player serves about 6 feet from center mark. Players at each end must be alert to serves being hit from the opposing side.
2. Each player should hit five serves into the designated area.
3. Shot difficulty can be increased as players warm up.

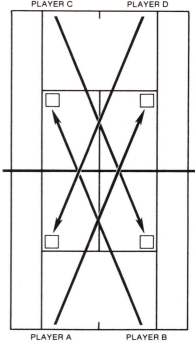

Figure 6-5. Serve Drill.

SERVE — APPROACH — VOLLEY

Purpose

To warm up the muscular system with strokes used in match play.

Drill

1. **A** serves with maximum of 50% power and gingerly moves to the net.
2. **B** returns serve down the middle.
3. **A** hits an approach shot that can be returned.
4. **B** returns down the middle.
5. **A** volleys for a winner.
6. **A** should hit 10 balls into play before becoming the receiver.
7. This can be used with 4 players. The 2 additional players begin as the first 2 finish.

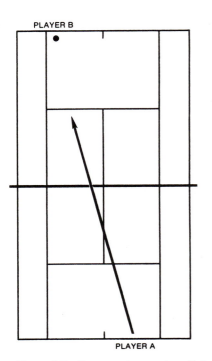

Figure 6-6. Serve — Approach — Volley.

SKILL TESTS

DYER TENNIS TEST This test is one of the earliest used to classify ability. T-score values developed with college women appeared in the Research Quarterly in 1938. It measures the number of hits against a backboard within a thirty-second period.

The test is given on a wall or backboard that is 10 feet high and about 15 feet wide. A three inch line is drawn 3 feet from the floor to represent the net. A line is drawn five feet from the base of the wall to represent the restraining line. Several balls should be placed conveniently for the player.

The object of the test is to hit the ball against the backboard (above the net line) as many times as possible during a thirty second period.

To begin the test the ball is dropped to put it in play. The ball must be played from behind the restraining line. Balls hit while the player is past the line do not count. If the player loses the ball, another one may be used. The new ball is put in play as the first one.

The test is scored by awarding one point for each hit above the net line during the thirty second limit. Each subject is given three trials. The highest total score is recorded.

BROER-MILLER TEST

Female players were used in this test to eliminate relative weakness and strength in the forehand and backhand drive. The test is designed for a specified number of balls to be hit above the net, but below a restraining rope stretched four feet above the net.

Chalk lines are drawn ten feet inside the service line and nine feet outside the service line. Two chalk lines are drawn behind the baseline five feet and 10 feet respectively. The numbers in the areas designate the scoring value.

The player being tested stands behind the base line, bounces the ball and attempts to place them in the back nine feet of the opposite court. Each player is allowed fourteen trials on the forehand and fourteen on the backhand. To score the values indicated in Figure 6-7, the balls must pass between the net and rope. Balls going over the rope are scored at half value. A ball missed is counted as a trial. Let balls are played over.

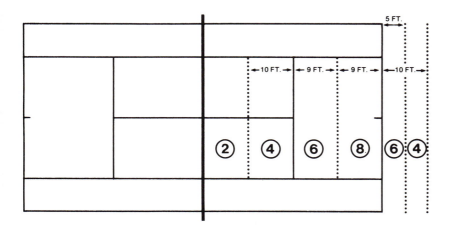

Figure 6.7. Broer-Miller Test.

KEMP-VINCENT RALLY TEST*   The purpose of this test is to measure achievement in tennis skill and to classify players by rally ability. Rally ability is determined according to player performance in a simulated tennis game.

Directions   Two players assume opposing positions on a singles court. On the starting signal, one of the players bounces a ball from behind the base line and puts it in play with a courtesy stroke. The players then proceed to keep the ball in play for three minutes. A ball hit into the net or out of bounds temporarily halts play until one of the players puts another ball into play. It is put into play in the same manner as was used to start the rally test. The use of any tennis stroke is permissible.

Four balls should be ready for use at the outset of the test. When these balls are used, the players must retrieve their own balls for the remainder of the test.

An error by a player refers to:

1. Failure to put the ball in play with a courtesy stroke.
2. Failure to hit the ball over the net in a rally.
3. Failure to put a new ball in play from behind the baseline.
4. Failure to keep the ball within the singles court area.
5. Failure to hit the ball before the second bounce.

As in singles tennis, balls hitting the boundary lines are in play, and those that strike the top of the net and land in bounds on the opponent's side are also playable. Balls landing out of bounds may be played at the discretion of the players for time-saving purposes.

Scoring Method   Initially, the total number of hits for the two players are counted, including those in which errors are committed. A courtesy stroke constitutes a hit. From the combined total hits of the two players, each subtracts his/her number of errors to determine the final rally score.

---

* From J. Kemp and M.F. Vincent, "Kemp-Vincent Rally Test of Tennis Skill," *Research Quarterly*, 39:1000-1004, 1968.

BEGINNING TENNIS SKILLS TEST

Name _____   **Date** _____

Section _____   **Time** _____

60 POSSIBLE POINTS

30 GROUNDSTROKES — Hitter stands behind the baseline.

Forehands (15)
Tosser stands halfway
between net and service line.

Forehands

Backhands (15)
Must toss **overhand** —
any bad toss does not have to be hit.

Backhands

10 VOLLEYS — Hitter stands halfway between net and service line.

Forehands (5)
Tosser stands halfway between net
and service line.

Forehands

Backhands (5)
Must toss underhand — any bad toss
does not have to be hit. Award 1 full
point if the ball lands behind the
service line, and one-half point if it
lands in front of the service line.

Backhands

20 SERVES — Let serves must be served again if they land in the proper court. If they land
out of the service box, it is a fault.

Deuce Court

Ad Court

I hereby certify that the above scores are correct.

1 _____   **2** _____   **3** _____

INTERMEDIATE TENNIS SKILLS TEST

Name _____ **Date** _____

Section _____ **Time** _____

30 POSSIBLE POINTS

8 GROUNDSTROKES — Hitters and tossers take same position as in Beginning Tennis.

Forehands (4)
Tosser can feed with racket or toss at hitter's preference.

Forehands

Backhands (4)
Balls landing in front of the service line are worth one-half point, one point for those landing behind the service line.

Backhands

6 VOLLEYS — Same as groundstrokes except hitter stands halfway between the net and service line.

Forehands (3)

Backhands (4)

16 SERVES — To receive one full point the serves must land past the baseline on the second bounce, one-half point for those landing in front of the baseline.

Deuce Court (8)

Ad Court (8)

I hereby certify that the above scores are correct.

1 _____ **2** _____ **3** _____

Special Topics

CHAPTER 7

SO YOU WANT TO TRY THE WESTERN FOREHAND

The success of Borg, Agassi and others have unfortunately caused a number of players to imitate this Western style. This grip is approximately one-quarter turn from the Eastern Forehand or one-half turn from the backhand. The knuckle of the thumb is on the beveled edge of the grip.

The major function of the Western grip is the tremendous topspin placed in the ball. The player is able to rally consistently and with power from the baseline. The ball clears the net three to four feet to give sufficient margin for error, then is pulled down by the topspin to land deep in the opponent's court.

Many "Western players" have trouble developing a well-rounded game. The open stance causes the ball to be hit two to three feet behind the contact point of the more orthodox Eastern grip. As a result, more miss-hits occur. The awkward grip change that must be made with an approach shot or low volley simply costs the player too many lost points.

THE LEFT-HANDER HAS THE ADVANTAGE

Only a few years ago, Rod Laver was the only left-hander playing professional tennis. Most instructors wanted to change the left-hander to a right-hander. They theorized that play was too difficult or more players would adapt to that style. I suspect the instructor did not want to think "the wrong way around." Fortunately, we have been enlightened to the contrary. Hundreds of outstanding players have emerged to dispel this erroneous theory. In fact, several Grand Slam champions are left-handed.

The proportion of left-handers to right-handers is low. This helps tremendously, because right-handers play between themselves and are unaccustomed to the opposite spins of the left-hander. The balls hit by a left-hander come from an unexpected direction and at a different angle. Unless the opposing player has plenty of experience, it will take a set or two to adjust to the different behavior of the ball. The spinning services and unusual volleys really confuse the opponents.

HOW TO WATCH TENNIS

When observing a crowd watching tennis, notice their heads swinging back and forth. Enough to cause a headache! Most spectators could probably give the score, but have little idea of how the players are performing.

One should observe the players, one at a time. Watching the individual player live or on TV can be a positive learning experience. You can determine excellent racket preparation watching Jennifer Capriati, Fred Stolle, Pete Sampras and others. Observe the follow-through. When the racket head finishes high on the ground stroke, the shot has topspin. When it finishes low, below the chest, it has slice or backspin. When it finishes between the two, it is relatively flat.

When observing one serve, do you watch the ball, or the position of the racket head after contact? What happens to the ball when the racket follows through across the body? What happens to the racket on a twist serve? Is the server trying to make the ball break wider toward the outside or break inward? Where is the receiver standing when a high bouncing spin serve is hit? Did the receiver chip the serve or stroke it? Was the point won because of good shot? Could the player losing the point have avoided the loss? How?

Critical observation of such movements can best be made above net level from the end position rather than the side position.

MIXED DOUBLES CAN BE FUN

This is a true statement if you are playing with somebody else's spouse or friend. Married couples are usually holy terrors in mixed doubles. Exasperation and disgust become dominant factors. Engagements are broken and divorce papers have been served by those who play doubles together.

Most mixed doubles conflicts develop from the male side of a team. He wants to take all the difficult shots. He believes he can save every point. Therefore, he tires out and the shots are hit to the female. She had better be alert.

The key is to allow each to play the ball at their own position. The team should utilize the female quickness at the net and the physical strength of the male in the back court.

PLAYING ETIQUETTE

Tennis is a game in which good manners and consideration of others is a tradition. Players and spectators with "class" follow these traditions.

▶ Spectators are quiet and respectful of the player's concentration during a point.

▶ This respectfulness is exhibited by moving to the restroom or concession stand only when players are changing sides of the court.

▶ Applause is appropriate when either player hits a good shot, but only after the point is completed.

Unwritten Etiquette for the Players

▶ Greet your opponent and introduce yourself.

▶ Spin for serve or court.

▶ Check the net height for accuracy. A standard size racket will measure 36 inches.

▶ Practice serves during warm-up before the match starts.

▶ Play should be continuous.

▶ Begin play as the server when you have two balls. One may be placed in a pocket or under the panties.

▶ Observe that your opponent is ready before serving.

▶ The server should call the score after each point. If the ball was in the court on a close line call, inform your opponent by turning the palm of the hand down (Figure 7-1). Point the index finger outside the court when ball is out (Figure 7-2).

▶ Each player is responsible for line decisions in his/her half of the court. When a point is in doubt, confer with opponent or request that the point be replayed.

Figure 7-1. Close Line Call — point good.

Figure 7-2. Close Line Call — ball out.

▶ Return only balls that are good, particularly on the serve.

▶ When you are not sure if a ball is in or out, play it as good and say nothing.

▶ Collect the balls on your side of the court after a point is played and return them to the server. In doubles play, the server's net partner holds the third ball.

▶ Retrieve balls from nearby courts after the point is over. You may then say, "Thank you" or "Ball please."

▶ Return balls to a nearby court only after their point is complete.

▶ Leave your court at the conclusion of play so that those waiting are not delayed.

▶ Honor the dress code of the tennis center during your match.

TENNIS CAN CONTRIBUTE TO YOUR WELL-BEING

For many years physical educators and tennis professionals have asserted that participation in sports would assure favorable outcomes for the players. The tenant of this statement is still true.

The correlation of mental and physical skill has been well documented by researchers, and we use tennis competition as an active medium for developing physical skills, concentration and mental acuity.

Successful playing involves the analysis of the opponent's strengths and weaknesses, as well as your own. Effective results are brought about by incorporating the analysis of the total game. In tennis, the player relies on his own mental alertness and skill. There are no time outs, no substitutions or talks with the coach. The effective player becomes aware of the limitless possibilities for improvement, perseverance, and courage.

It is an activity which also provides opportunities for the player to develop control of the emotions in a highly emotional situation. In a close match, decisions are made by the player which can dramatically alter the results. This internal desire to be fair is a mark of integrity, exhibited by great professional and amateur players. I have observed professionals ask the umpire for a decision change which favored the opponent. On numerous occasions, I have been present at amateur tournaments in which a player was awarded a victory by default, because the opponent failed to appear at the match deadline. Later, when the opponent arrived, the player who won by default, asked the tournament referee for a decision change to play the match. The opponent won the match, and the winner became the loser, or did he? An individual with integrity on the athletic field displays integrity in life.

PROGRAM YOUR CONCENTRATION

We were at the university playing on Court One. I was taking a pretty good thrashing when two female friends of my opponent walked up to watch. Subconsciously, he wanted to exhibit a flaw-less game, but instead, developed an endless flow of distracting thoughts. He lost the match.

When you become too concerned about what others think or consciously try to please other people; when you become too sensitive to the approval or disapproval of others, then you have negative feedback, inhibition, and poor performance. If we consciously (in match play) concern ourselves with trying harder to make a good impression, we become inhibited and self-conscious.

Conscious effort inhibits and jams our success mechanism. A skilled drummer could never play a simple piece if he tried to consciously think of just which stick would strike which drum while he is playing. He thought about it previously while learning and practiced until the actions became automatic.

Tennis strokes are often programmed into bits and pieces that confuse and frustrate even the most well-adjusted player. If we try (while in a match) to remember each point taught by the instructor, we become too tense, too anxious, and too concerned for results. Concentration is totally interrupted. The time for concern with these basics is during instruction and drill periods. These skills must become a part of you during the match.

The practice sessions are for programming. In match play, "press the key," then let it happen. Execute the basic techniques which have been mastered. Creative performance is spontaneous and natural as opposed to self-conscious and critical.

Relaxing and maintaining a relaxed attitude helps remove excessive concern, tension and anxiety which interfere with the efficient operation of your success mechanism.

Concentration is the act of focusing attention and one can reach his/her limits when he achieves it. Practice and grow until you reach maximum physical and mental effort. The realization that you are using maximum effort will transcend beyond the anxieties.

INDIVIDUAL GOALS AND TEAM ENTHUSIASM

Forget yesterday's failures and concentrate on the successes of today. When you anticipate success, you achieve success.

We have observed numerous teams which possessed that intangible quality of team spirit. There seems to be a closeness or cohesiveness that lifts the team to a higher quality. There is almost a magical quality which is exhibited by a special courage and perseverance. They feel the winning attitude. They turn crisis into opportunity and see adversity as a challenge. A team with this internal enthusiasm will often defeat a team which is clearly superior. Perhaps the principles listed below will aid you in establishing this state of well-being:

1. Realize that your principle goal as a player is to play and be happy and that confidence is a state of happiness that is a goal in itself.

2. Confidence means positive thinking, positive action and trying. You must have great desire, a feeling of enthusiasm, that you can reach the goal. Imagine that you are already there.

3. Think in terms of success. When you feel successful, you will act with confidence.

4. Reactivate your thinking process to relive the confidence of the past.

5. Relive a successful experience. One's mind cannot tell the difference between a true experience and one vividly imagined.

6. Accept negative feelings of your game as a challenge. Confidence is the capacity to rise above this negative attitude.

7. Substitute a good feeling of confidence for a bad feeling of frustration. Make it a habit.

8. Confidence comes from a belief in yourself. The belief comes from an active performance, not a passive wish.

9. Rise above your failures to reach a full measure of dignity.

10. When you have a goal, you prepare for success.

YOU WANT TO CHANGE YOUR GAME

You should write on paper the parts of your game which offer the greatest success. Write down the mistakes most often made in your last match. Use various techniques discussed earlier in this book to reduce the errors encountered. Experiment with new skills, techniques and drills that contribute to success. Watch tennis on TV. Determine the changes which might contribute to your style of play. Ask a pro to observe your play in a competition situation. Some constructive changes should be apparent by following these suggestions.

Appendix

NATIONAL TENNIS RATING PROGRAM

Occasionally, players find it difficult to rate or judge their own abilities. Some underestimate, but more overestimate. Because of this dilemma, tennis professionals developed a rating program. The National Tennis Rating Program was introduced by the USTA, USPTA and the NTA. The program identifies thirteen brief classifications. Each describes a recognized level of play. Select one that most accurately describes your level of play. If you cannot decide between two ratings, place yourself in the lower one.

Beginning 1.0-2.0
Intermediate .2.5-3.5
Advanced. 4.0-4.5
Tournament Player 5.0-5.5
Wins Tournaments 6.0
Top Amateur or Pro 6.5-7.0

To Place Yourself:

A. Begin with 1.0. Read all categories carefully and then decide which one best describes your present ability level.

B. Be certain that you qualify on all points of all preceding categories as well as those in the classification you choose.

C. When rating yourself assume you are playing against a player of the same sex and the same ability.

D. Your self rating may be verified by a teaching professional, coach, league chairman or other qualified expert.

E. The person in charge of your tennis program has the right to reclassify you if your self placement is thought to be inappropriate.

1.0 This player is just starting to play the game of tennis.

1.5 This player has limited playing experience and is still working primarily on getting the ball over the net; has some knowledge of scoring but is familiar with basic positions and procedures for singles and doubles play.

2.0 This player may have had some lessons but needs on court experience; has obvious stroke weaknesses but is beginning to feel comfortable with singles and doubles play.

2.5 This player has more dependable strokes and is learning to judge where the ball is going; has weak court coverage or is often caught out of position, but is starting to keep the ball in play with other players of the same ability.

3.0 This player can place shots with moderate success; can sustain a rally of slow pace but is not comfortable with all strokes; lacks control when trying for power.

3.5 This player has achieved stroke dependability and direction on shots within reach, including forehand and backhand volleys but still lacks depth and variety; seldom double faults and occasionally forces errors on the serve.

4.0 This player has dependable strokes on both forehand and backhand sides; has the ability to use a variety of shots, including lobs, overheads, approach shots and volleys; can place the first serve and force some errors; is seldom out of position in a doubles game.

4.5 This player has begun to master the use of power and spins; has sound footwork; can control depth of shots and is able to move opponent up and back; can hit first serves with power and accuracy and place the second serve; is able to rush net with some success on serve in singles as well as doubles.

5.0 This player has good shot anticipation; frequently has an outstanding shot or exceptional consistency around which a game may be structured; can regularly hit winners or force errors off of short balls; can successfully execute lobs, drop shots, half volleys and overhead smashes; has good depth and spin on most second serves.

5.5 This player can execute all strokes offensively and defensively; can hit dependable shots under pressure; is able to analyze opponents' styles and can employ patterns of play to assure the greatest possibility of winning points; can hit winners or force errors with both first and second serves. Return of serves can be an offensive weapon.

6.0 This player has mastered all of the above skills; has developed power and/or consistency as a major weapon; can vary strategies and styles of play in a competitive situation. This player typically has had intensive training for national competition at junior or collegiate levels.

6.5 This player has mastered all of the above skills and is an experienced tournament competitor who regularly travels for competition and whose income may be partially derived from prize winnings.

7.0 This is a world class player.

SKILL PROBLEMS

On the space provided at the bottom of each photo, identify the incorrect technique and write the necessary changes.

1

_____

_____

2

_____

_____

3

_____

_____

4

_____

_____

5
_____

_____

6
_____

_____

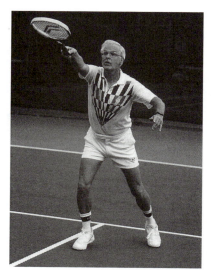

7
_____

_____

8
_____

_____

9

_____

_____

10

_____

_____

11

_____

_____

12

_____

_____

INTRODUCTION AND ORIENTATION
FOR A TENNIS CLASS

Tennis is a fun game. It is an activity which improves one's finest level, developes stamina and hopefully lifts one's mental attitude. This text is designed to continue the quest for fun and greater release from stress. The instruction techniques are brief and to the point. Each player should find a key word, a drill or some new techniques which will contribute positively to a lifetime of tennis.

The instructor for this course is _____

Course Title _____ Days Meeting _____ Time._____

LOCKER FACILITIES AND CLOTHING

Men's Locker Room is located _____

Women's Locker Room is located_____

Regulation tennis shoes and appropriate tennis attire are REQUIRED. Most tennis instructors determine student grades by skill performance and knowledge obtained. The instructor will inform each student of the procedures used to make scores on the written test and improve performance, strategy and technique. Letter grades shown have values on a scale of 100 points.

A	Excellent	90–100
B	Good	80–89
C	Average	70–79
D	Poor	60–69
F	Failure	59 and below

WEATHER

Instruction will be on court _____

Should inclement conditions develop (the instructor will define those) class will meet in

_____

Each player will meet during the instructional period, regardless of weather.

Talk with your instructor should an emergency prevent you from attending an instructional period.

Glossary Of Terms

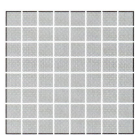

ACE   A serve so fast or so sharply angled (or both) that the receiver is unable to make contact.

ADVANTAGE   The game score when the server wins the point immediately after deuce.

AD COURT   The left service court

AD IN   The game score when the server wins the point immediately after deuce. Same as advantage.

AD OUT   The game score when the receiver wins the point immediately after deuce.

ALL   Referring to tied scores, such as 4 all in the set score (each player has won 4 games) or 30 all in the game score (each player has won 2 points in that game).

ALLEY   A 4-foot lane on both sides of the single court. This enlarged width is used only in doubles.

AMERICAN TWIST   An advanced player's serve that has a combination of top spin and side spin. A right-handed server, the ball will bounce high and to the right. A left-handed server, the ball will bounce high and to the left.

ANGLE SHOT   A shot that is hit sharply cross-court.

APPROACH   A ground stroke hit by the player moving to the net.

ATP   Association of Tennis Professionals. The governing body of male tennis professionals.

ATTACK   An aggressive shot hit from a given position.

AUSTRALIAN DOUBLES   A position in doubles play where the net player lines up on the same side as the server.

BACK COURT   The area between the service line and base line. The area is often referred to as "no man's land."

BACKHAND   The stroke used to play a ball on the left side of a right-handed player or the right side of a left-handed player.

BACKHAND COURT   The left side of the court for a right handed player or the right side of the court for a left handed player.

BACKSPIN   Backward spin on the ball, with the top of the ball rotating away from its direction of flight. Sometimes referred to as underspin, slice or chop.

BACKSWING   The beginning part of a swing before ball contact. Should not exceed 180 degrees.

BALL BOY   One who retrieves balls for tennis players during competition. Also a commercial ball retriever used by pros to pick up balls after instruction.

BASE LINE   The line farthest from the net on each end of the court located thirty-nine feet from the net.

BREAK   (Service break) To win a game the opponent serves.

BORON   An extremely strong, "stiff like", "metal like" material used in racket construction.

CANNONBALL SERVE   A very hard hit flat serve.

CARRY   An illegal hit which causes the ball to be slung or hit twice before crossing the net.

CENTER MARK   The short line that bisects the center of the base line.

CENTER SERVICE LINE   Perpendicular line to the net which divides the two service courts.

CENTER STRAP   A strap at the center of the net attached to a metal hook to hold the net secure.

CERAMIC   A space age material of high strength and durability. Less than ten percent of this material is used in racket construction.

CHIP   A partial slice, generally used in doubles on a service return. A chip requires little racket swing.

CHOKE   To grip the racket upward from the handle. Also, increased stress and reduced ability during competition.

CHOP   A backspin shot caused by a downward (45 degree) movement of the racket.

CLOSED FACE   The angle of the hitting face of the racket when it is turned down toward the surface.

CLOSED TOURNAMENT   A tournament open only to a participant of a specified area or group.

CONSOLATION   A tournament in which a first round loser may continue to play in a losers bracket.

CONTINENTAL GRIP   A grip that is measured one quarter turn to the left of an eastern forehand. Some players used this grip to hit all shots.

CROSS COURT SHOT   A shot in which the ball travels diagonally across the net from one corner to the other.

CYCLOPS   An electronic device that sounds when a serve is outside the line. It is used only in major tournaments.

DEAD BALL   A ball that has lost its resiliency. It bounces improperly. A normal ball will bounce 53–58 inches when dropped from a height of 100 inches.

DEFAULT   Failure to appear or complete a scheduled match in a tournament, such player loses the match.

DEUCE   A tie score of 40–40 and anytime thereafter when the score is tied in the same game.

DEUCE COURT   The right service court viewed from one's own base line.

DINK   A softly hit shot which makes the opponent run, usually hit with spin.

DOUBLE FAULT   Failure of the server to hit either of the two service attempts into the proper court.

DOUBLE ELIMINATION   A tournament in which one must lose twice before being eliminated.

DOUBLES   Match play with two players on each side.

DOWN THE LINE   A shot hit parallel to the side line.

DRAW   A procedure established to determine the position of each player in a tournament.

DRIVE   A shot hit with enough force to win the point or cause a weak return.

DROP SHOT   A softly hit ball with backspin that clears the net and lands near the net.

DROP VOLLEY   A drop shot that is hit from a volley.

EASTERN GRIP   The grip used by the majority of players for hitting the forehand. Sometimes called the "shake hands grip."

ERROR An unintentional mistake which results in a lost point.

FACE Strings or hitting surface of the racket.

FAST COURT Generally a hard surfaced court, which allows the tennis ball to bounce quickly and low.

FAULT The failure to serve a ball in the proper service court.

FEDERATION CUP International team competition for women. Two singles matches and one doubles match constitute a team match. A nation must win at least two of the three matches to advance to the next round.

FIBERGLASS A flexible glass fiber used with other materials in racket construction.

FIFTEEN The first point won by a player in a game. (Inexperienced players often refer to this point as five).

FLAT SHOT A shot which has little spin. It may resemble a drive with less force.

FLOATER A ball (with little spin) hit to the opposing side in a high trajectory.

FOOT FAULT An illegal serve caused by the server stepping on or over the base line before hitting the ball.

FORECOURT The area between the service line and net.

FOREHAND The stroke used to return balls hit from the dominant side of a player.

FOREHAND COURT The right side of the court for a right-handed player; left side for a left-handed player.

FORTY The player's score after winning three points.

FRAME Any part of the racket except the strings.

GAME That portion of a set completed when one player or side wins four points, or wins two consecutive points after deuce.

GRAND SLAM An outstanding accomplishment of tournament wins in a single year which include the French Open, The Australian Open, Wimbledon and U.S. Open. These are considered to be the major tennis events in the world.

GRAPHITE A carbon-based material that is approximately twenty times stronger than wood. First used to strengthen aircraft wings. It is now a standard material used in racket construction.

GRIP The covering of the handle. The method of holding a racket.

GROMMET A small round plastic sleeve in the frame through which the strings pass.

GROUND STROKE A forehand or backhand stroke hit after the ball has bounced.

GUT Tournament strings made from lamb, sheep or beef intestines.

HACKER A tennis player with limited skills and form.

HALF VOLLEY The ball is hit or blocked immediately after it bounces.

HANDLE The lower part of the racket that is gripped in the hand.

HEAD The part of the racket used to hit the ball, includes the frame and strings.

HOLD SERVICE An expression used when a game is won by the server.

I T F International Tennis Federation — the governing organization for tennis throughout the world.

KEVLAR A synthetic high tech fiber used to strengthen racket frames.

LET Any point that must be replayed because of interference.

LET SERVE The occasion when a serve hits the top of the net and lands in the proper service court. (*See* LET)

LINESMAN One who is designated to call balls that land outside the line during competition.

LOB A ball hit high enough to pass over the head of the opposing player and move that player back to the base line.

LOB VOLLEY *See* volley. A high, softly hit shot over the head of an opponent that rushes the net.

LOVE No score. zero.

LOVE GAME In a love game, no points are scored by the losing side.

LOVE SET In a love set, no games are won by the losing side.

MATCH A contest which one team must win two of three sets. In some championship matches, one team must win three of five sets.

MATCH POINT The final point needed to win the match.

MIXED DOUBLES Male and female player composing one team in doubles.

MID COURT The general area in the center of the playing court expanding four to six feet from the center service line.

NET GAME A player who generally advances to the forecourt to make an offensive volley.

NET MAN The partner in doubles who plays at the net.

NO ADD SCORING See VASSS. Scoring that requires the winner to have four points.

NO MANS LAND The area located at midcourt to the baseline, where the ball bounces at the players feet. Regarded as a poor area for developing ball control.

NOT-UP The same as a double bounce which is a loss of point.

OPEN FACE The angle of the racket face when it is turned up toward the sky.

OUT A ball which lands outside the playing court.

OVERHEAD or SMASH A stroke used for a ball hit overhead. Placement rather than force.

PACE The speed of the ball; usually with topspin.

PASSING SHOT A ball hit past the opponent on either side.

POACH This strategy is used in doubles. The net player instinctively leaves the normal position, crosses in front of his partner to steal the ball for a quick point.

PRO-SET A pro-set is used to shorten a match. A player or team must win (8) eight games and be ahead by at least two games.

RALLY A series of shots hit consecutively without missing.

ROUND ROBIN A tournament in which each player or team plays each of the other players or teams.

RUSH A player moving to the net after hitting an approach shot.

SEED An arrangement of tournament matches that allows top players to play lesser opponents in early rounds.

SEMI WESTERN GRIP A baseline players grip. Place the hand on the racket for an eastern forehand, then move the hand about one quarter turn to the right.

SERVE The stroke used to put the ball into play at the beginning of each point.

SERVICE BREAK A game won by the receiver.

SERVICE LINE The line at the base of the service court; parallel to the baseline and twenty-one feet from the net.

SET A unit of a match. A side must win six games and be two games ahead or win the tie breaker.

SET POINT The point which, if won, decides the winner of the set.

SHORT TENNIS A teaching concept initiated on a short court. U.S.T.A., in a pilot program, found that children's gross motor skills can be transferred more easily with this concept.

SIDE SPIN   A shot which causes the ball to spin sideward or on its vertical axis.

SINGLES   A match between two players.

SLICE SEE CHIP   A backspin shot hit with the racket moving down through the ball at angles generally less than forty-five degrees.

SLOW COURT   A court with an abrasive or rough surface which causes the ball to bounce high and slower.

SMASH   *See* Overhead.

SPIN   Spin on the ball caused by hitting it at an angle or off center.

SPLIT SETS   When each player has won one set and a third set decides the winner of the match.

STOP VOLLEY   Same as drop volley.

STRAIGHT SETS   The winner of the match won all sets played.

SUDDEN DEATH   *See* Tiebreaker.

SWEET SPOT   The area of the racket strings or racket face that produces controlled power with little or no vibration.

TAPE   A white band across the top of the net.

TAKE TWO   A cool expression meaning take two serves.

TENNIS ELBOW   A painful condition of the elbow brought about from a variety of factors.

THIRTY   A score which indicates a player has won two points.

THROAT   The part of the racket between the handle and racket face.

TIE BREAKER   A scoring system to eliminate long sets. When a set becomes tied at six games each, players may elect to play a 5 of 9 or a 7 of 12 point tie breaking game.

TOPSPIN   A forward spin, with the top of the ball rotating in the direction of its flight.

USTA   United States Tennis Association; the organization that governs tennis in the U.S.; formerly U.S.L.T.A.

UMPIRE   A person who officiates at matches.

UNDERCUT   A backspin caused by hitting down through the ball.

UNDERSPIN   *See* Chop, Backspin.

UNSEEDED   Players that are not expected to win a tournament. Positions are established by chance.

VASSS   Van Alen Simplified Scoring System. No ad scoring of 1-2-3-game. The first player to win four points wins the game.

VOLLEY   A ball hit before it bounces, usually hit in the forecourt.

WCT   World Championship Tennis. A professional tournament played throughout the world. The top eight players met in Dallas each April to determine the championship.

WESTERN GRIP   Move the hand another quarter turn to the right from the semi-western grip.

WIDE BODY   This is a broader racket when viewed from the side. It is the newest technology in rackets. See "rackets" in the section on choosing your equipment.

WIGHTMAN CUP   An annual tournament of female players representing the U.S. and England.

WITA   Women's International Tennis Association was developed to improve prize money, pension plans, tournament schedules, player rankings, player health and conditions of play.

WORLD TEAM TENNIS   Franchise organization composed of the world's best male and female players.

WOOD SHOT   (maybe called frame shot) A ball hit on the wood of the racket.

WTA Women's Tennis Association is an organization of professional female tennis players. WTA also denotes World Tennis Association consisting of the world's best female professional players.

United States Tennis Association Rules of Tennis

Rules of Tennis

Explanatory Note

The following Rules and Cases and Decisions are the official Code of the International Tennis Federation, of which the United States Tennis Association is a member. USTA Comments have the same weight and force in USTA tournaments as do ITF Cases and Decisions.

When a match is played without officials the principles and guidelines set forth in the USTA Publication, The Code, shall apply in any situation not covered by the rules.

Except where otherwise stated, every reference in these Rules to the masculine includes the feminine gender.

The Singles Game

RULE 1

The Court

The court shall be a rectangle 78 feet (23.77m.) long and 27 feet (8.23m.) wide.

USTA Comment: *See Rule 34 for a doubles court.*

It shall be divided across the middle by a net suspended from a cord or metal cable of a maximum diameter of one-third of an inch (0.8cm.), the ends of which shall be attached to, or pass over, the tops of two posts, which shall be not more than 6 inches (15cm.) square or 6 inches (15cm.) in diameter. These posts shall not be higher than 1 inch (2.5 cm.) above the top of the net cord. The centres of the posts shall be 3 feet (0.914m.) outside the court on each side and the height of the posts shall be such that the top of the cord or metal cable shall be 3 feet 6 inches (1.07m.) above the ground.

When a combined doubles (see Rule 34) and singles court with a doubles net is used for singles, the net must be supported to a height of 3 feet 6 inches (1.07m.) by means of two posts, called "singles sticks", which shall be not more than 3 inches (7.5cm.) square or 3 inches (7.5cm.) in diameter. The centres of the singles sticks shall be 3 feet (0.914m.) outside the singles court on each side.

The net shall be extended fully so that it fills completely the space between the two posts and shall be of sufficiently small mesh to prevent the ball passing through. The height of the net shall be 3 feet (0.914m.) at the centre, where it shall be held down taut by a strap not more than 2 inches (5cm.) wide and completely white in colour. There shall be a band covering the cord or metal cable and the top of the net of not less than 2 inches (5cm.) nor more than 2½ inches (6.3cm.) in depth on each side and completely white in colour.

There shall be no advertisement on the net, strap, band or singles sticks.

The lines bounding the ends and sides of the Court shall respectively be called the base-lines and the side-lines. On each side of the net, at a distance of 21 feet (6.40m.) from it and parallel with it, shall be drawn the service-lines. The space on each side of the net between the service-line and the side-lines shall be divided into two equal parts called the service-courts by the centre service-line, which must be 2 inches (5cm.) in width, drawn half-way between, and parallel with, the side-lines. Each base-line shall be bisected by an imaginary continuation of the centre service-line to a line 4 inches (10cm.) in length and 2 inches (5cm.) in width called the centre mark drawn inside the Court, at right angles to and in contact with such base-lines. All other lines shall be not less than 1 inch (2.5cm.) nor more than 2 inches (5cm.) in width, except the base-line, which may be not more than 4 inches (10cm.) in width, and all measurements shall be made to the outside of the lines. All lines shall be of uniform colour.

If advertising or any other material is placed at the back of the court, it may not contain white, or yellow. A light colour may only be used if this does not interfere with the vision of the players.

If advertisements are placed on the chairs of the Linesmen sitting at the back of the court, they may not contain white, or yellow. A light colour may only be used if this does not interfere with the vision of the players.

ITF Note: In the case of the *Davis Cup* or other Official Championships of the International Tennis Federation, there shall be a space behind each base-line of not less than 21 feet (6.4m.), and at the sides of not less than 12 feet (3.66m.). The chairs of the linesmen may be placed at the back of the court within the 21 feet or at the side of the court within the 12 feet, provided they do not protrude into that area more than 3 feet (.914m).

USTA Comment: *An approved method for obtaining proper net tautness is this: Loosen the center strap; tighten the net cord until it is approximately 40 inches above the ground, being careful not to overtighten the net; tighten the center strap until the center of the net is 36 inches above the ground. These measurements should always be made before the first match of the day. For a plan of the court see the preceding diagram.*

RULE 2

Permanent Fixtures

The permanent fixtures of the Court shall include not only the net, posts, singles sticks, cord or metal cable, strap and band, but also, where there are any such, the back and side stops, the stands, fixed or movable seats and chairs round the Court, and their occupants, all other fixtures around and above the Court, and the Umpire, Net-cord Judge, Foot-fault Judge, Linesmen and Ball Boys when in their respective places.

ITF Note: For the purpose of this Rule, the word "Umpire" comprehends the Umpire, the persons entitled to a seat on the Court, and all those persons designated to assist the Umpire in the conduct of a match.

RULE 3

The Ball

The ball shall have a uniform outer surface and shall be white or yellow in colour. If there are any seams, they shall be stitchless.

The ball shall be more than two and a half inches (6.35cm.) and less than two and five-eighths inches (6.67cm.) in diameter, and more than two ounces (56.7 grams) and less than two and one-sixteenth ounces (58.5 grams) in weight.

The ball shall have a bound of more than 53 inches (135cm.) and less than 58 inches (147cm.) when dropped 100 inches (254cm.) upon a concrete base.

The ball shall have a forward deformation of more than .220 of an inch (.56cm.) and less than .290 of an inch (.74cm.) and a return deformation of more than .350 of an inch (.89cm.) and less than .425 of an inch (1.08cm.) at 18 lb. (8.165kg.) load. The two deformation figures shall be the averages of three individual readings along three axes of the ball and no two individual readings shall differ by more than .030 of an inch (.08cm.) in each case.

For play above 4,000 feet (1219m) in altitude above sea level, two additional types of ball may be used. The first type is identical to those described above except that the bound shall be more than 48 inches (121.92cm.) and less than 53 inches (135cm) and the ball shall have an internal pressure that is greater than the external pressure. This type of tennis ball is commonly known as a pressurized ball. The second type is identical to those described above except that they shall have a bound of more than 53 inches (135cm) and less than 58 inches (147cm) and shall have an internal pressure that is approximately equal to the external pressure and have been acclimatized for 60 days or more at the altitude of the specific tournament. This type of tennis ball is commonly known as a zero-pressure or non-pressurized ball.

All tests for bound, size and deformation shall be made in accordance with the Regulations in the Appendix hereto.

RULE 4
The Racket
Rackets failing to comply with the following specifications are not approved for play under the Rules of Tennis:

(a) The hitting surface of the racket shall be flat and consist of a pattern of crossed strings connected to a frame and alternately interlaced or bonded where they cross; and the stringing pattern shall be generally uniform, and in particular not less dense in the centre than in any other area. The strings shall be free of attached objects and protrusions other than those utilized solely and specifically to limit or prevent wear and tear or vibration and which are reasonable in size and placement for such purposes.

(b) The frame of the racket shall not exceed 32 inches (81.28cm.) in overall length, including the handle and 12½ inches (31.75cm.) in overall width. The strung surface shall not exceed 15½ inches (39.37cm.) in overall length, and 11½ inches (29.21cm.) in overall width.

(c) The frame, including the handle, shall be free of attached objects and devices other than those utilized solely and specifically to limit or prevent wear and tear or vibration, or to distribute weight. Any objects and devices must be reasonable in size and placement for such purposes.

(d) The frame, including the handle and the strings, shall be free of any device which makes it possible to change materially the shape of the racket, or to change the weight distribution, during the playing of a point.

The International Tennis Federation shall rule on the question of whether any racket or prototype complies with the above specifications or is otherwise approved, or not approved, for play. Such ruling may be undertaken on its own initiative, or upon application by any party with a bona fide interest therein, including any player, equipment manufacturer or National Association or members thereof. Such rulings and applications shall be made in accordance with the applicable Review and Hearing Procedures of the International Tennis Federation, copies of which may be obtained from the office of the Secretary.

Case 1. Can there be more than one set of strings on the hitting surface of a racket?
Decision. No. The rule clearly mentions a pattern, and not patterns, of crossed strings.
Case 2. Is the stringing pattern of a racket considered to be generally uniform and flat if the strings are on more than one plane?
Decision. No.
Case 3. Can a vibration dampening device be placed on the strings of a racket and if so, where can it be placed?
Decision. Yes; but such devices may only be placed outside the pattern of crossed strings.

RULE 5
Server and Receiver
The players shall stand on opposite sides of the net; the player who first delivers the ball shall be called the Server, and the other the Receiver.

Case 1. Does a player, attempting a stroke, lose the point if he crosses an imaginary line in the extension of the net,
(a) before striking the ball,
(b) after striking the ball?
Decision. He does not lose the point in either case by crossing the imaginary line and provided he does not enter the lines bounding his opponent's Court (Rule 20 (e)). In regard to hindrance, his opponent may ask for the decision of the Umpire under Rules 21 and 25.
Case 2. The Server claims that the Receiver must stand within the lines bounding his Court. Is this necessary?
Decision. No. The Receiver may stand wherever he pleases on his own side of the net.

RULE 6
Choice of Ends and Service
The choice of ends and the right to be Server or Receiver in the first game shall be decided by toss. The player winning the toss may choose or require his opponent to choose:

(a) The right to be Server or Receiver, in which case the other player shall choose the end; or

(b) The end, in which case the other player shall choose the right to be Server or Receiver.

USTA Comment: *These choices should be made promptly after the toss and are irrevocable, except that if the match is postponed or suspended before the start of the match. See Case 1 below.*

Case 1. Do players have the right to new choices if the match is postponed or suspended before it has started?
Decision. Yes. The toss stands, but new choices may be made with respect to service and end.

RULE 7
The Service
The service shall be delivered in the following manner. Immediately before commencing to serve, the Server shall stand with both feet at rest behind (i.e. further from the net than) the base-line, and within the imaginary continuations of the centre-mark and side-line. The Server shall then project the ball by hand into the air in any direction and before it hits the ground strike it with his racket, and the delivery shall be deemed to have been completed at the moment of the impact of the racket and the ball. A player with the use of only one arm may utilize his racket for the projection.

USTA Comment: *The service begins when the Server takes a ready position (i.e., both feet at rest behind the baseline) and ends when his racket makes contact with the ball, or when he misses the ball in attempting to serve it.*

Case 1. May the Server in a singles game take his stand behind the portion of the base-line between the side-lines of the Singles Court and the Doubles Court?
Decision. No.

USTA Comment: *The server may stand anywhere in back of the baseline between the imaginary extensions of the center mark and the singles sideline.*

Case 2. If a player, when serving, throws up two or more balls instead of one, does he lose that service?
Decision. No. A let should be called, but if the Umpire regards the action as deliberate he may take action under Rule 21.

USTA Comment: *There is no restriction regarding he kind of service which may be used; that is, the player may use an underhand or overhand service at his discretion.*

RULE 8
Foot Fault
(a) The Server shall throughout the delivery of the service:

(i) Not change his position by walking or running. The Server shall not by slight movements of the feet which do not materially affect the location originally taken up by him, be deemed "to change his position by walking or running".

(ii) Not touch, with either foot, any area other than that behind the base-line within the imaginary extensions of the centre mark and side-lines.

(b) The word "foot" means the extremity of the leg below the ankle.

USTA Comment: *This rule covers the most decisive stroke in the game, and there is no justification for its not being obeyed by players and enforced by officials. No official has the right to instruct any umpire to disregard violations of it. In a non-officiated match, the Receiver, or his partner, may call foot faults after all efforts (appeal to the server, request for an umpire, etc.) have failed and the foot faulting is so flagrant as to be clearly perceptible from the Receiver's side.*

It is improper for any official to warn a player that he is in danger of having a foot fault called on him. On the other hand, if a player, in all sincerity, asks for an explanation of how he foot faulted, either the Line Umpire or the Chair Umpire should give him that information.

RULE 9
Delivery of Service
(a) In delivering the service, the Server shall stand alternately behind the right and left Courts beginning from the right in every game. If service from a wrong half of the Court occurs and is undetected, all play resulting from such wrong service or services shall stand, but the inaccuracy of station shall be corrected immediately it is discovered.

(b) The ball served shall pass over the net and hit the ground within the Service Court which is diagonally opposite, or upon any line bounding such Court, before the Receiver returns it.

USTA Comment: *See Rule 18.*

RULE 10

Service Fault

The Service is a fault:

(a) If the Server commits any breach of Rules 7, 8 or 9(b);

(b) If he misses the ball in attempting to strike it;

(c) If the ball served touches a peramanent fixture (other than the net, strap or band) before it hits the ground.

Case 1. After throwing a ball up preparatory to serving, the Server decides not to strike at it and catches it instead. Is it a fault?

Decision. No.

USTA Comment: As long as the Server makes no attempt to strike the ball, it is immaterial whether he catches it in his hand or on his racket or lets it drop to the ground.

Case 2. In serving in a singles game played on a Doubles Court with doubles posts and singles sticks, the ball hits a singles stick and then hits the ground within the lines of the correct Service Court. Is this a fault or a let?

Decision. In serving it is a fault, because the singles stick, the doubles post, and that portion of the net, or band between them are permanent fixtures. (Rules 2 and 10, and note to Rule 24.)

USTA Comment: *The significant point governing Case 2 is that the part of the net and band "outside" the singles sticks is not part of the net over which this singles match is being played. Thus such a serve is a fault under the provisions of Article (c) above . . . By the same token, this would be a fault also if it were a singles game played with permanent posts in the singles position. (See Case 1 under Rule 24 for difference between "service" and "good return" with respect to a ball's hitting a net post.)*

USTA Comment: *In a non-officiated singles match, each player makes calls for all balls landing on, or aimed at, his side of the net. In doubles, normally the Receiver's partner makes the calls with respect to the service line, with the Receiver calling the side and center lines, but either partner may make the call on any ball he clearly sees out.*

RULE 11

Second Service

After a fault (if it is the first fault) the Server shall serve again from behind the same half of the Court from which he served that fault, unless the service was from the wrong half, when, in accordance with Rule 9, the Server shall be entitled to one service only from behind the other half.

Case 1. A player serves from a wrong Court. He loses the point and then claims it was a fault because of his wrong station.

Decision. The point stands as played and the next service should be from the correct station according to the score.

Case 2. The point score being 15 all, the Server, by mistake, serves from the left-hand Court. He wins the point. He then serves again from the right-hand Court, delivering a fault. This mistake in station is then discovered. Is he entitled to the previous point? From which Court should he next serve?

Decision. The previous point stands. The next service should be from the left-hand Court, the score being 30/15, and the Server has served one fault.

RULE 12

When To Serve

The Server shall not serve until the Receiver is ready. If the latter attempts to return the service, he shall be deemed ready. If, however, the Receiver signifies that he is not ready, he may not claim a fault because the ball does not hit the ground within the limits fixed for the service.

USTA Comment: *The Server must wait until the Receiver is ready for the second service as well as the first, and if the Receiver claims to be not ready and does not make any effort to return a service, the Server's claim for the point may not be honored even though the service was good. However, the Receiver, having indicated he is ready, may not become unready unless some outside interference takes place.*

RULE 13

The Let

In all cases where a let has to be called under the rules, or to provide for an interruption to play, it shall have the following interpretations:

(a) When called solely in respect of a service that one service only shall be replayed.

(b) When called under any other circumstance, the point shall be replayed.

Case 1. A service is interrupted by some cause outside those defined in Rule 14. Should the service only be replayed?

Decision. No, the whole point must be replayed.

USTA Comment: *If a delay between first and second serves is caused by the Receiver, by an official or by an outside interference the whole point shall be replayed; if the delay is caused by the Server, the Server has one serve to come. A spectator's outcry (of "out", "fault" or other) is not a valid basis for replay of a point, but action should be taken to prevent a recurrence.*

USTA Comment: *Case 1 refers to a second serve, and the decision means that if the interruption occurs during delivery of the second service, the Server gets two serves. Example: On a second service a linesman calls "fault" and immediately corrects it, the Receiver meanwhile having let the ball go by. The Server is entitled to two serves, on this ground: The corrected call means that the Server has put the ball into play with a good service, and once the ball is in play and a let is called, the point must be replayed. Note, however, that if the serve is an unmistakable ace — that is, the Umpire is sure the erroneous call had no part in the Receiver's inability to play the ball — the point should be declared for the Server.*

Case 2. If a ball in play becomes broken, should a let be called?

Decision. Yes.

USTA Comment: *A ball shall be regarded as having become "broken" if, in the opinion of the Chair Umpire, it is found to have lost compression to the point of being unfit for further play, or unfit for any reason, and it is clear the defective ball was the one in play.*

RULE 14

The "Let" in Service

The service is a let:

(a) If the ball served touches the net, strap or band, and is otherwise good, or, after touching the net, strap or band, touches the Receiver or anything which he wears or carries before hitting the ground.

(b) If a service or a fault is delivered when the Receiver is not ready (see Rule 12).

In case of a let, that particular service shall not count, and the Server shall serve again, but a service let does not annul a previous fault.

RULE 15

Order of Service

At the end of the first game the Receiver shall become Server, and the Server Receiver; and so on alternately in all the subsequent games of a match. If a player serves out of turn, the player who ought to have served shall serve as soon as the mistake is discovered, but all points scored before such discovery shall be reckoned. If a game shall have been completed before such discovery, the order of service remains as altered. A fault served before such discovery shall not be reckoned.

RULE 16

When Players Change Ends

The players shall change ends at the end of the first, third and every subsequent alternate game of each set, and at the end of each set unless the total number of games in such set is even, in which case the change is not made until the end of the first game of the next set.

If a mistake is made and the correct sequence is not followed the players must take up their correct station as soon as the discovery is made and follow their original sequence.

RULE 17

The Ball in Play

A ball is in play from the moment at which it is delivered in service. Unless a fault or a let is called it remains in play until the point is decided.

USTA Comment: *A point is not decided simply when, or because, a good shot has clearly passed a player, or when an apparently bad shot passes over a baseline or sideline. An outgoing ball is still definitely in play until it actually strikes the ground, backstop or a permanent fixture (other than the net, posts, singles sticks, cord or metal cable, strap or band), or a player. The same applies to a good ball, bounding after it has landed in the proper court. A ball that becomes imbedded in the net is out of play.*

Case 1. A player fails to make a good return. No call is made and the ball remains in play. May his opponent later claim the point after the rally has ended?

Decision. No. The point may not be claimed if the players continue to play after the error has been made, provided the opponent was not hindered.

USTA Comment: *To be valid, an out call on A's shot to B's court, that B plays, must be made before B's shot has either gone out of play or has been hit by A. See Case 3 under Rule 29.*

USTA Comment: *When a ball is hit into the net and the player on the other side, thinking the ball is coming over, strikes at it and hits the net he loses the point if his touching the net occurs while the ball is still in play.*

RULE 18

Server Wins Point

The Server wins the point:

(a) If the ball served, not being a let under Rule 14, touches the Receiver or anything which he wears or carries, before it hits the ground;

(b) If the Receiver otherwise loses the point as provided by Rule 20.

RULE 19

Receiver Wins Point

The Receiver wins the point:

(a) If the Server serves two consecutive faults;

(b) If the Server otherwise loses the point as provided by Rule 20.

RULE 20

Player Loses Point

A player loses the point if:

(a) He fails, before the ball in play has hit the ground twice consecutively, to return it directly over the net (except as provided in Rule 24(a) or (c)); or

(b) He returns the ball in play so that it hits the ground, a permanent fixture, or other object, outside any of the lines which bound his opponent's Court (except as provided in Rule 24(a) or (c)); or

USTA Comment: *A ball hitting a scoring device or other object attached to a net post results in loss of point to the striker.*

(c) He volleys the ball and fails to make a good return even when standing outside the Court; or

(d) In playing the ball he deliberately carries or catches it on his racket or deliberately touches it with his racket more than once; or

USTA Comment: *Only when there is a definite "second push" by the player does his shot become illegal, with consequent loss of point. The word 'deliberately' is the key word in this rule. Two hits occurring in the course of a single continuous swing are not deemed a double hit.*

(e) He or his racket (in his hand or otherwise) or anything which he wears or carries touches the net, posts, singles sticks, cord or metal cable, strap or band, or the ground within his opponent's Court at any time while the ball is in play; or

USTA Comment: *Touching a pipe support that runs across the court at the bottom of the net is interpreted as touching the net; See USTA Comment under Rule 23.*

(f) He volleys the ball before it has passed the net; or

(g) The ball in play touches him or anything that he wears or carries, except his racket in his hand or hands; or

USTA Comment: *This loss of point occurs regardless of whether the player is inside or outside the bounds of his court when the ball touches him.*

(h) He throws his racket at and hits the ball; or

(i) He deliberately and materially changes the shape of his racket during the playing of the point.

Case 1. In serving, the racket flies from the Server's hand and touches the net before the ball has touched the ground. Is this a fault, or does the player lose the point?

Decision. The Server loses the point because his racket touches the net whilst the ball is in play (Rule 20 (e)).

Case 2. In serving, the racket flies from the Server's hand and touches the net after the ball has touched the ground outside the proper court. Is this a fault, or does the player lose the point?

Decision. This is a fault because the ball was out of play when the racket touched the net.

Case 3. A and B are playing against C and D, A is serving to D, C touches the net before the ball touches the ground. A fault is then called because the service falls outside the Service Court. Do C and D lose the point?

Decision. The call "fault" is an erroneous one. C and D had already lost the point before "fault" could be called, because C touched the net whilst the ball was in play (Rule 20 (e)).

Case 4. May a player jump over the net into his opponent's Court while the ball is in play and not suffer penalty?

Decision. No. He loses the point (Rule 20 (e)).

Case 5. A cuts the ball just over the net, and it returns to A's side. B, unable to reach the ball, throws his racket and hits the ball. Both racket and ball fall over the net on A's Court. A returns the ball outside of B's Court. Does B win or lose the point?

Decision. B loses the point (Rule 20 (e) and (h)).

Case 6. A player standing outside the service Court is struck by a service ball before it has touched the ground. Does he win or lose the point?

Decision. The player struck loses the point (Rule 20 (g)), except as provided under Rule 14 (a).

Case 7. A player standing outside the Court volleys the ball or catches it in his hand and claims the point because the ball was certainly going out of court.

Decision. In no circumstances can he claim the point:

(1) If he catches the ball he loses the point under Rule 20 (g).

(2) If he volleys it and makes a bad return he loses the point under Rule 20 (c).

(3) If he volleys it and makes a good return, the rally continues.

RULE 21

Player Hinders Opponent

If a player commits any act which hinders his opponent in making a stroke, then, if this is deliberate, he shall lose the point or if involuntary, the point shall be replayed.

USTA Comment: *'Deliberate' means a player did what he intended to do, although the resulting effect on his opponent might or might not have been what he intended. Example: a player, after his return is in the air, gives advice to his partner in such a loud voice that his opponent is hindered. 'Involuntary' means a non-intentional act such as a hat blowing off or a scream resulting from a sudden wasp sting.*

Case 1. Is a player liable to a penalty if in making a stroke he touches his opponent?

Decision. No, unless the Umpire deems it necessary to take action under Rule 21.

Case 2. When a ball bounds back over the net, the player concerned may reach over the net in order to play the ball. What is the ruling if the player is hindered from doing this by his opponent?

Decision. In accordance with Rule 21, the Umpire may either award the point to the player hindered, or order the point to be replayed. (See also Rule 25).

Case 3. Does an involuntary double hit constitute an act which hinders an opponent within Rule 21?

Decision. No.

USTA Comment: *Upon appeal by a competitor that the server's action in discarding a "second ball" after a rally has started constitutes a distraction (hindrance), the Umpire, if he deems the claim valid, shall require the server to make some other and satisfactory disposition of the ball. Failure to comply with this instruction may result in loss of point(s) or disqualification.*

RULE 22

Ball Falls on Line

A ball falling on a line is regarded as falling in the Court bounded by that line.

USTA Comment: *In a non-officiated singles match, each player makes the call on any ball hit toward his side of the net, and if a player cannot call a ball out with surety he should regard it as good. See paragraph 7 of The Code and the last USTA Comment under Rule 10.*

RULE 23

Ball Touches Permanent Fixtures

If the ball in play touches a permanent fixture (other than the net, posts, singles sticks, cord or metal cable, strap or band) after it has hit the ground, the player who struck it wins the point; if before it hits the ground, his opponent wins the point.

Case 1. A return hits the Umpire or his chair or stand. The player claims that the ball was going into Court.

Decision. He loses the point.

USTA Comment: *A ball in play that after passing the net strikes a pipe support running across the court at the base of the net is regarded the same as a ball landing on clear ground. See also Rule 20(e).*

RULE 24

A Good Return

It is a good return:

(a) If the ball touches the net, posts, singles sticks, cord or metal cable, strap or band, provided that it passes over any of them and hits the ground within the Court; or

(b) If the ball, served or returned, hits the ground within the proper Court and rebounds or is blown back over the net, and the player whose turn it is to strike reaches over the net and plays the ball, provided that he does not contravene Rule 20(e).

(c) If the ball is returned outside the posts, or singles sticks, either above or below the level of the top of the net, even though it touches the posts or singles sticks, provided that it hits the ground within the proper Court; or

(d) If a player's racket passes over the net after he has returned the ball, provided the ball passes the net before being played and is properly returned; or

(e) If a player succeeds in returning the ball, served or in play, which strikes a ball lying in the Court.

USTA Comment: *Paragraph (e) of the rule refers to a ball lying on the court at the start of the point, as a result of a service let or fault, or as a result of a player dropping it. If a ball in play strikes a rolling or stationary "foreign" ball that has come from elsewhere after the point started, a let should be played. See Case 7 under Rule 25 and note that it pertains to an object other than a ball that is being used in the match.*

ITF Note: In a singles match, if, for the sake of convenience, a doubles court is equipped with singles sticks for the purpose of a singles game, then the doubles posts and those portions of the net, cord or metal cable and the band outside such singles sticks shall at all times be permanent fixtures, and are not regarded as posts or parts of the net of a singles game.

A return that passes under the net cord between the singles stick and adjacent doubles post without touching either net cord, net or doubles post and falls within the court, is a good return.

USTA Comment: *But in doubles this would be a "through" — loss of point.*

Case 1. A ball going out of Court hits a net post or singles stick and falls within the lines of the opponent's Court. Is the stroke good?

Decision. If a service: no, under Rule 10 *(c)*. If other than a service: yes, under Rule 24 *(a)*.

Case 2. Is it a good return if a player returns the ball holding his racket in both hands?

Decision. Yes.

Case 3. The service, or ball in play, strikes a ball lying in the Court. Is the point won or lost thereby?

USTA Comment: *A ball that is touching a boundary line is considered to be "lying in the court".*

Decision. No. Play must continue. If it is not clear to the Umpire that the right ball is returned a let should be called.

Case 4. May a player use more than one racket at any time during play?

Decision. No; the whole implication of the Rules is singular.

Case 5. May a player request that a ball or balls lying in his opponent's Court be removed?

Decision. Yes, but not while a ball is in play.

RULE 25

Hindrance of a Player

In case a player is hindered in making a stroke by anything not within his control, except a permanent fixture of the Court, or except as provided for in Rule 21, a let shall be called.

Case 1. A spectator gets into the way of a player, who fails to return the ball. May the player then claim a let?

Decision. Yes, if in the Umpire's opinion he was obstructed by circumstances beyond his control, but not if due to permanent fixtures of the Court or the arrangements of the ground.

Case 2. A player is interfered with as in Case No. 1, and the Umpire calls a let. The Server had previously served a fault. Has he the right to two services?

Decision. Yes: as the ball is in play, the point, not merely the stroke, must be replayed as the Rule provides.

Case 3. May a player claim a let under Rule 25 because he thought his opponent was being hindered, and consequently did not expect the ball to be returned?

Decision. No.

Case 4. Is a stroke good when a ball in play hits another ball in the air?

Decision. A let should be called unless the other ball is in the air by the act of one of the players, in which case the Umpire will decide under Rule 21.

Case 5. If an Umpire or other judge erroneously calls "fault" or "out", and then corrects himself, which of the calls shall prevail?

Decision. A let must be called unless, in the opinion of the Umpire, neither player is hindered in his game, in which case the corrected call shall prevail.

Case 6. If the first ball served — a fault — rebounds, interfering with the Receiver at the time of the second service, may the Receiver claim a let?

Decision. Yes. But if he had an opportunity to remove the ball from the Court and negligently failed to do so, he may not claim a let.

Case 7. Is it a good stroke if the ball touches a stationary or moving object on the Court?

Decision. It is a good stroke unless the stationary object came into Court after the ball was put into play in which case a let must be called. If the ball in play strikes an object moving along or above the surface of the Court a let must be called.

Case 8. What is the ruling if the first service is a fault, the second service correct, and it becomes necessary to call a let either under the provision of Rule 25 or if the Umpire is unable to decide the point?

Decision. The fault shall be annulled and the whole point replayed.

USTA Comment: *See Rule 13 with its USTA Comments.*

RULE 26

Score in a Game

If a player wins his first point, the score is called 15 for that player; on winning his second point, the score is called 30 for that player; on winning his third point, the score is called 40 for that player, and the fourth point won by a player is scored game for that player except as below:

If both players have won three points, the score is called deuce; and the next point won by a player is scored advantage for that player. If the same player wins the next point, he wins the game; if the other player wins the next point the score is again called deuce; and so on, until a player wins the two points immediately following the score at deuce, when the game is scored for that player.

USTA Comment: *In a non-officiated match the Server should announce, in a voice audible to his opponent and spectators, the set score at the beginning of each game, and point scores as the game goes on. Misunderstandings will be avoided if this practice is followed.*

RULE 27

Score in a Set

(a) A player (or players) who first wins six games wins a set; except that he must win by a margin of two games over his opponent and where necessary a set is extended until this margin is achieved.

(b) The tie-break system of scoring may be adopted as an alternative to the advantage set system in paragraph (a) of this Rule provided the decision is announced in advance of the match.

USTA Comment: *See the Tie-Break System near the middle of this book.*

In this case, the following Rules shall be effective:

The tie-break shall operate when the score reaches six games all in any set except in the third or fifth set of a three set or five set match respectively when an ordinary advantage set shall be played, unless otherwise decided and announced in advance of the match.

The following system shall be used in a tie-break game.

Singles

(i) A player who first wins seven points shall win the game and the set provided he leads by a margin of two points. If the score reaches six points all the game shall be extended until this margin has been achieved. Numerical scoring shall be used throughout the tie-break game.

(ii) The player whose turn it is to serve shall be the server for the first point. His opponent shall be the server for the second and third points and thereafter each player shall serve alternately for two consecutive points until the winner of the game and set has been decided.

(iii) From the first point, each service shall be delivered alternately from the right and left courts, beginning from the right court. If service from a wrong half of the court occurs and is undetected, all play resulting from such wrong service or services shall stand, but the inaccuracy of station shall be corrected immediately it is discovered.

(iv) Players shall change ends after every six points and at the conclusion of the tie-break game.

(v) The tie-break game shall count as one game for the ball change, except that, if the balls are due to be changed at the beginning of the tie-break, the change shall be delayed until the second game of the following set.

Doubles

In doubles the procedure for singles shall apply. The player whose turn it is to serve shall be the server for the first point. Thereafter each player shall serve in rotation for two points, in the same order as previously in that set, until the winners of the game and set have been decided.

Rotation of Service

The player (or pair in the case of doubles) whose turn it was to serve first in the tie-break game shall receive service in the first game of the following set.

Case 1. At six all the tie-break is played, although it has been decided and announced in advance of the match that an advantage set will be played. Are the points already played counted?

Decision. If the error is discovered before the ball is put in play for the second point, the first point shall count but the error shall be corrected immediately. If the error is discovered after the ball is put in play for the second point the game shall continue as a tie-break game.

Case 2. At six all, an advantage game is played, although it has been decided and announced in advance of the match that a tie-break will be played. Are the points already played counted?

Decision. If the error is discovered before the ball is put in play for the second point, the first point shall be counted but the error shall be corrected immediately. If the error is discovered after the ball is put in play for the second point an advantage set shall be continued. If the score thereafter reaches eight games all or a higher even number, a tie-break shall be played.

Case 3. If during a tie-break in a singles or doubles game, a player serves out of turn, shall the order of service remain as altered until the end of the game?

Decision. If a player has completed his turn of service the order of service shall remain as altered. If the error is discovered before a player has completed his turn of service the order of service shall be corrected immediately and any points already played shall count.

RULE 28

Maximum Number of Sets

The maximum number of sets in a match shall be 5, or, where women take part, 3.

RULE 29

Role of Court Officials

In matches where an Umpire is appointed, his decision shall be final; but where a Referee is appointed, an appeal shall lie to him from the decision of an Umpire on a question of law, and in all such cases the decision of the Referee shall be final.

In matches where assistants to the Umpire are appointed (Linesmen, Net-cord Judges, Foot-fault Judges) their decisions shall be final on questions of fact except that if in the opinion of an Umpire a clear mistake has been made he shall have the right to change the decision of an assistant or order a let to be played. When such an assistant is unable to give a decision he shall indicate this immediately to the Umpire who shall give a decision. When an Umpire is unable to give a decision on a question of fact he shall order a let to be played.

In Davis Cup matches or other team competitions where a Referee is on Court, any decision can be changed by the Referee, who may also instruct an Umpire to order a let to be played.

The Referee, in his discretion, may at any time postpone a match on account of darkness or the condition of the ground or the weather. In any case of postponement the previous score and previous occupancy of Courts shall hold good, unless the Referee and the players unanimously agree otherwise.

USTA Comment: *See second USTA Comment under Rule 30.*

Case 1. The Umpire orders a let, but a player claims that the point should not be replayed. May the Referee be requested to give a decision?

Decision. Yes. A question of tennis law, that is an issue relating to the application of specific facts, shall first be determined by the Umpire. However, if the Umpire is uncertain or if a player appeals from his determination, then the Referee shall be requested to give a decision, and his decision is final.

Case 2. A ball is called out, but a player claims that the ball was good. May the Referee give a ruling?

Decision. No. This is a question of fact, that is an issue relating to what actually occurred during a specific incident, and the decision of the on-court officials is therefore final.

Case 3. May an Umpire overrule a Linesman at the end of a rally if, in his opinion, a clear mistake has been made during the course of a rally?

Decision. No, unless in his opinion the opponent was hindered. Otherwise an Umpire may only overrule a Linesman if he does so immediately after the mistake has been made.

USTA Comment: *See Rule 17, Case 1.*

Case 4. A Linesman calls a ball out. The Umpire was unable to see clearly, although he thought the ball was in. May he overrule the Linesman?

Decision. No. An Umpire may only overrule if he considers that a call was incorrect beyond all reasonable doubt. He may only overrule a ball determined good by a Linesman if he has been able to see a space between the ball and the line; and he may only overrule a ball determined out, or a fault, by a Linesman if he has seen the ball hit the line, or fall inside the line.

Case 5. May a Linesman change his call after the Umpire has given the score?

Decision. Yes. If a Linesman realises he has made an error, he may make a correction provided he does so immediately.

Case 6. A player claims his return shot was good after a Linesman called "out". May the Umpire overrule the Linesman?

Decision. No. An Umpire may never overrule as a result of a protest or an appeal by a player.

RULE 30
Continuous Play and Rest Periods

Play shall be continuous from the first service until the match is concluded, in accordance with the following provisions:

(a) If the first service is a fault, the second service must be struck by the Server without delay.

The Receiver must play to the reasonable pace of the Server and must be ready to receive when the Server is ready to serve.

When changing ends a maximum of one minute thirty seconds shall elapse from the moment the ball goes out of play at the end of the game to the time the ball is struck for the first point of the next game.

The Umpire shall use his discretion when there is interference which makes it impractical for play to be continuous.

The organizers of international circuits and team events recognized by the ITF may determine the time allowed between points, which shall not at any time exceed 25 seconds.

USTA Comment: *In USTA sanctioned tournaments, a maximum of 25 seconds shall elapse from the moment the ball goes out of play at the end of one point to the time the ball is struck for the next point.*

(b) Play shall never be suspended, delayed or interfered with for the purpose of enabling a player to recover his strength, breath, or physical condition.

However, in the case of accidental injury, the Umpire may allow a one-time three minute suspension for that injury.

The organizers of international circuits and team events recognized by the ITF may extend the one-time suspension period from three minutes to five minutes.

(c) If, through circumstances outside the control of the player, his clothing, footwear or equipment (excluding racket) becomes out of adjustment in such a way that it is impossible or undesirable for him to play on, the Umpire may suspend play while the maladjustment is rectified.

USTA Comment: *Loss of, or damage to, a contact lens or eyeglasses shall be treated as equipment maladjustment. All players must follow the same rules with respect to suspending play, even though in misty, but playable, weather a player who wears glasses may be handicapped.*

(d) The Umpire may suspend or delay play at any time as may be necessary and appropriate.

USTA Comment: *When a match is resumed after a suspension of more than ten minutes, it is permissible for the players to engage in a re-warm-up that may be of the same duration as that at the start of the match. The preferred method is to warm-up with other used balls and then insert the match balls when play starts. If the match balls are used in the re-warm-up, then the next ball change will be two games sooner. There shall be no re-warm-up after an authorized intermission or after a suspension of ten minutes or less.*

(e) After the third set, or when women take part the second set, either player is entitled to a rest, which shall not exceed 10 minutes, or in countries situated between latitude 15 degrees north and latitude 15 degrees south, 45 minutes and furthermore, when necessitated by circumstances not within the control of the players, the Umpire may suspend play for such a period as he may consider necessary. If play is suspended and is not resumed until a later day the rest may be taken only after the third set (or when women take part the second set) of play on such a later day, completion of an unfinished set being counted as one set.

If play is suspended and is not resumed until 10 minutes have elapsed in the same day the rest may be taken only after three consecutive sets have been played without interruption (or when women take part two sets), completion of an unfinished set being counted as one set.

Any nation and/or committee organizing a tournament, match or competition, other than the International Tennis Championships (Davis Cup and Federation Cup), is at liberty to modify this provision or omit it from its regulations provided this is announced before the event commences.

(f) A tournament committee has the discretion to decide the time allowed for a warm-up period prior to a match but this may not exceed five minutes and must be announced before the event commences.

USTA Comment: *When there are no ballpersons this time may be extended to 10 minutes.*

(g) When approved point penalty and non-accumulative point penalty systems are in operation, the Umpire shall make his decisions within the terms of those systems.

(h) Upon violation of the principle that play shall be continuous the Umpire may, after giving due warning, disqualify the offender.

RULE 31
Coaching

During the playing of a match in a team competition, a player may receive coaching from a captain who is sitting on the court only when he changes ends at the end of a game, but not when he changes ends during a tie-break game.

A player may not receive coaching during the playing of any other match.

After due warning an offending player may be disqualified. When an approved point penalty system is in operation, the Umpire shall impose penalties according to that system.

Case 1. Should a warning be given, or the player be disqualified, if the coaching is given by signals in an unobtrusive manner?

Decision. The Umpire must take action as soon as he becomes aware that coaching is being given verbally or by signals. If the Umpire is unaware that coaching is being given, a player may draw his attention to the fact that advice is being given.

Case 2. Can a player receive coaching during an authorized rest period under Rule 30(e), or when play is interrupted and he leaves the court?

Decision. Yes. In these circumstances, when the player is not on the court, there is no restriction on coaching.

ITF Note: The word "coaching" includes any advice or instruction.

RULE 32
Changing Balls

In cases where balls are to be changed after a specified number of games, if the balls are not changed in the correct sequence, the mistake shall be corrected when the player, or pair in the case of doubles, who should have served with new balls is next due to serve. Thereafter the balls shall be changed so that the number of games between changes shall be that originally agreed.

RULE 33
The Doubles Game

The above Rules shall apply to the Doubles Game except as below.

RULE 34

The Doubles Court

For the Doubles Game, the Court shall be 36 feet (10.97m.) in width, i.e. 4½ feet (1.37m.) wider on each side than the Court for the Singles Game, and those portions of the singles side-lines which lie between the two service-lines shall be called the service side-lines. In other respects, the Court shall be similar to that described in Rule 1, but the portions of the singles side-lines between the base-line and service-line on each side of the net may be omitted if desired.

USTA Comment: *The Server has the right in doubles to stand anywhere back of the baseline between the center mark imaginary extension and the doubles sideline imaginary extension.*

RULE 35

Order of Service in Doubles

The order of serving shall be decided at the beginning of each set as follows:

The pair who have to serve in the first game of each set shall decide which partner shall do so and the opposing pair shall decide similarly for the second game. The partner of the player who served in the first game shall serve in the third; the partner of the player who served in the second game shall serve in the fourth, and so on in the same order in all the subsequent games of a set.

Case 1. In doubles, one player does not appear in time to play, and his partner claims to be allowed to play single-handed against the opposing players. May he do so?

Decision. No.

RULE 36

Order of Receiving in Doubles

The order of receiving the service shall be decided at the beginning of each set as follows:

The pair who have to receive the service in the first game shall decide which partner shall receive the first service, and that partner shall continue to receive the first service in every odd game throughout that set. The opposing pair shall likewise decide which partner shall receive the first service in the second game and that partner shall continue to receive the first service in every even game throughout that set. Partners shall receive the service alternately throughout each game.

Case 1. Is it allowable in doubles for the Server's partner or the Receiver's partner to stand in a position that obstructs the view of the Receiver?

Decision. Yes. The Server's partner or the Receiver's partner may take any position on his side of the net in or out of the Court that he wishes.

RULE 37

Service Out of Turn in Doubles

If a partner serves out of his turn, the partner who ought to have served shall serve as soon as the mistake is discovered, but all points scored, and any faults served before such discovery, shall be reckoned. If a game shall have been completed before such discovery, the order of service remains as altered.

USTA Comment: *For an exception to Rule 37 see Case 3 under Rule 27.*

RULE 38

Error in Order of Receiving in Doubles

If during a game the order of receiving the service is changed by the Receivers it shall remain as altered until the end of the game in which the mistake is discovered, but the partners shall resume their original order of receiving in the next game of that set in which they are Receivers of the service.

RULE 39

Service Fault in Doubles

The service is a fault as provided for by Rule 10, or if the ball touches the Server's partner or anything which he wears or carries; but if the ball served touches the partner of the Receiver, or anything which he wears or carries, not being a let under Rule 14(a) before it hits the ground, the Server wins the point.

RULE 40

Playing the Ball in Doubles

The ball shall be struck alternately by one or other player of the opposing pairs, and if a player touches the ball in play with his racket in contravention of this Rule, his opponents win the point.

USTA Comment: *This means that, in the course of making one return, only one member of a doubles team may hit the ball. If both of them hit the ball, either simultaneously or consecutively, it is an illegal return. The partners themselves do not have to "alternate" in making returns. Mere clashing of rackets does not make a return illegal unless it is clear that more than one racket touched the ball.*

ITF Note: Except where otherwise stated, every reference in these rules to the masculine includes the feminine gender.

If you have a rules problem, send full details, enclosing a stamped self-addressed envelope, to USTA Tennis Rules Committee, c/o Umpires Department, 1212 Avenue of the Americas, New York, NY 10036.

APPENDIX I
Regulations for Making Tests Specified in Rule 3

1. Unless otherwise specified all tests shall be made at a temperature of approximately 68° Fahrenheit (20° Centigrade) and a relative humidity of approximately 60 per cent. All balls should be removed from their container and kept at the recognized temperature and humidity for 24 hours prior to testing, and shall be at that temperature and humidity when the test is commenced.

2. Unless otherwise specified the limits are for a test conducted in an atmospheric pressure resulting in a barometric reading of approximately 30 inches (76cm.).

3. Other standards may be fixed for localities where the average temperature, humidity or average barometric pressure at which the game is being played differ materially from 68° Fahrenheit (20° Centigrade), 60 per cent and 30 inches (76cm.) respectively.

Applications for such adjusted standards may be made by any National Association to the International Tennis Federation and if approved shall be adopted for such localities.

4. In all tests for diameter a ring gauge shall be used consisting of a metal plate, preferably non-corrosive, of a uniform thickness of one-eighth of an inch (.32cm.) in which there are two circular openings 2.575 inches (6.54cm.) and 2.700 inches (6.86cm.) in diameter respectively. The inner surface of the gauge shall have a convex profile with a radius of one-sixteenth of an inch. (.16cm.). The ball shall not drop through the smaller opening by its own weight and shall drop through the larger opening by its own weight.

5. In all tests for deformation conducted under Rule 3, the machine designed by Percy Herbert Stevens and patented in Great Britain under Patent No. 230250, together with the subsequent additions and improvements thereto, including the modifications required to take return deformations, shall be employed or such other machine which is approved by a National Association and gives equivalent readings to the Stevens machine.

6. Procedure for carrying out tests.

(a) Pre-compression. Before any ball is tested it shall be steadily compressed by approximately one inch (2.54cm.) on each of three diameters at right angles to one another in succession; this process to be carried out three times (nine compressions in all). All tests to be completed within two hours of precompression.

(b) Bound test (as in Rule 3). Measurements are to be taken from the concrete base to the bottom of the ball.

(c) Size test (as in paragraph 4 above).

(d) Weight test (as in Rule 3).

(e) Deformation test. The ball is placed in position on the modified Stevens machine so that neither platen of the machine is in contact with the cover seam. The contact weight is applied, the pointer and the mark brought level, and the dials set to zero. The test weight equivalent to 18 lb. (8.165kg.) is placed on the beam and pressure applied by turning the wheel at a uniform speed so that five seconds elapse from the instant the beam leaves its seat until the pointer is brought level with the mark. When turning ceases the reading is recorded (forward deformation). The wheel is turned again until figure ten is reached on the scale (one inch [2.54 cm.] deformation). The wheel is then rotated in the opposite direction at a uniform speed (thus releasing pressure) until the beam pointer again coincides with the mark. After waiting ten seconds the pointer is adjusted to the mark if necessary. The reading is then recorded (return deformation). This procedure is repeated on each ball across the two diameters at right angles to the initial position and to each other.